JOURNEY TO THE COMMON GOOD

UPDATED EDITION

Also by Walter Brueggemann
from Westminster John Knox Press

Abiding Astonishment: Psalms, Modernity, and the Making of History (Literary Currents in Biblical Interpretation series)

Cadences of Hope: Preaching among Exiles

Celebrating Abundance: Devotions for Advent

Chosen? Reading the Bible amid the Israeli-Palestinian Conflict

The Collected Sermons of Walter Brueggemann, vols. 1, 2, and 3

First and Second Samuel (Interpretation series)

From Judgment to Hope: A Study on the Prophets

From Whom No Secrets Are Hid: Introducing the Psalms

Genesis (Interpretation series)

Gift and Task: A Year of Daily Readings and Reflections

A Glad Obedience: Why and What We Sing

A Gospel of Hope

Great Prayers of the Old Testament

Hope for the World: Mission in a Global Context

Hope within History

Interrupting Silence: God's Command to Speak Out

An Introduction to the Old Testament: The Canon and Christian Imagination, Third Edition (with Tod A. Linafelt)

Isaiah 1–39 (Westminster Bible Companion series)

Isaiah 40–66 (Westminster Bible Companion series)

Living Countertestimony: Conversations with Walter Brueggemann (with Carolyn J. Sharp)

Mandate to Difference: An Invitation to the Contemporary Church

Many Voices, One God: Being Faithful in a Pluralistic World (with George W. Stroup)

Materiality as Resistance: Five Elements for Moral Action in the Real World

Money and Possessions (Interpretation Resources series)

Names for the Messiah: An Advent Study

An On-Going Imagination: A Conversation about Scripture, Faith, and the Thickness of Relationship (with Clover Reuter Beal)

Power, Providence, and Personality: Biblical Insight into Life and Ministry

Rebuilding the Foundations: Social Relationships in Ancient Scripture and Contemporary Culture (with John Brueggemann)

Reverberations of Faith: A Theological Handbook of Old Testament Themes

Sabbath as Resistance: Saying No to the Culture of Now, New Edition with Study Guide

Struggling with Scripture (with Brian K. Blount and William C. Placher)

Texts for Preaching: A Lectionary Commentary, Years A and B (with Charles B. Cousar, Beverly Roberts Gaventa, J. Clinton McCann, and James D. Newsome)

Truth and Hope: Essays for a Perilous Age

Truth Speaks to Power: The Countercultural Nature of Scripture

Using God's Resources Wisely: Isaiah and Urban Possibility

The Vitality of Old Testament Traditions, Second Edition (with Hans Walter Wolff)

A Way other than Our Own: Devotions for Lent (compiled by Richard Floyd)

JOURNEY TO THE COMMON GOOD

UPDATED EDITION

WALTER BRUEGGEMANN

WESTMINSTER
JOHN KNOX PRESS
LOUISVILLE · KENTUCKY

For Chris Graham

© 2010, 2021 Walter Brueggemann
First edition published 2010
Updated edition published 2021

Updated edition
Published by Westminster John Knox Press
Louisville, Kentucky

21 22 23 24 25 26 27 28 29 30—10 9 8 7 6 5 4 3 2 1

Book design by Drew Stevens
Cover design by Allison Taylor

Library of Congress Cataloging-in-Publication Data is on file at the Library of Congress, Washington, DC.

ISBN-13: 978-0-664-26731-5

CONTENTS

ACKNOWLEDGMENTS

I am pleased to acknowledge that the materials in this book, with some updates for this edition, constitute my 2008 Laing Lectures at Regent College, an occasion I remember with great delight. I was graciously hosted by John Stackhouse and Holly Rail, and I enjoyed the hospitality of other staff as well as students. I especially appreciated the companionship of Roger Laing, the donor whose generosity made the lectures possible.

Before these chapters reached their "final form" at Regent College, I made use of the materials in a preliminary form in several other venues. Readers may hear echoes from those preliminary presentations, most notably in chapter 2 via the General Synod of my church, the United Church of Christ. I am, as usual, grateful to Tia Foley, who completed the formulation and formatting of the chapters, and to Jon Berquist, the generous editor of the original edition of this book at Westminster John Knox Press. I am, with this updated edition, grateful to Julie Mullins for her careful discerning work on permitting this book to reappear.

I am glad to dedicate this book to Chris Graham, my colleague in ministry in the United Church of Christ. Chris practiced ministry with the kind of joy, courage, honesty, and freedom that properly belongs to gospel ministry. I am grateful to him as a partner in ministry and as a steadfast friend.

JOURNEY TO THE COMMON GOOD
A REINTRODUCTION

Within this book, I explore some ways in which Scripture—ancient text as authorizing word—may impinge on the faith and life and practice of the church as we journey together toward the common good that God wills for the world. The task of interpretation that gives contemporary access to the scriptural text is an ongoing one that is never finished. It requires, moreover, venturesome imagination that is always risky; those risks, however, are not as great as the risk of flat, one-dimensional reiteration that does not connect. I have returned to the theme of this book, "journey," and the interpretive risks necessary to it, in the midst of our current social crisis. (I write this on the day of the funeral in Houston for George Floyd, who was murdered by police in Minneapolis.) This crisis is deep, thick, and complex, but it has three faces of presentation:

- the virus that for now has outflanked our scientific capacity;
- the economic meltdown in the wake of the virus; and
- a skewed criminal justice system for which police misconduct is the visible front.

These three dimensions of the crisis together have a huge impact on the body politic:

- the virus leaves us variously *vulnerable* in its not-yet-understood danger;
- the economic meltdown leaves many people in deep *dislocation*; and
- the crisis in criminal justice evokes *anger and fear.*

When I thought about these poignant social realities of *vulnerability, dislocation, plus anger and fear,* it occurred to me that in the Bible the context that presents a similar lived experience is the wilderness sojourn of Israel after the slaves had departed Pharaoh's Egypt. Thus I suggest that in the face of our crisis, we may do well to consider the wilderness tradition in the Bible as a context in which faith may be powerfully pertinent. I allude to the wilderness narrative in the following chapters but give it little direct attention, and so wish to expand on it here. We in our current circumstance have an opportunity to bring that tradition close to our own experience, as we find ourselves on a particular journey of risk and responsibility. That narrative, I suggest, is marked by three remembered realities.

I.

Escape to the wilderness from Egypt meant that Israel had moved *beyond the reach and governance of Pharaoh.* His control did not extend to that untamed territory. This meant, for the newly emancipated slaves, that they were freed, at last, from the coercive demands of Pharaoh to serve his hunger for a monopoly of grain (see Gen 47:13–26 and James C. Scott, *Against the Grain*[1]). Pharaoh's require-

---

1. James C. Scott, *Against the Grain: A Deep History of the Earliest States* (New Haven, CT: Yale University Press, 2017).

ments were unending and insatiable (see Exod 5), and now the slaves no longer had to answer for unreasonable brick quotas, a harbinger first of unreasonable quotas for chopping cotton and current unreasonable requirements for meat-packing workers! It is no wonder that just as the slaves crossed the waters into the wilderness away from the reach of Pharaoh's demand economy that Miriam and the other women took tambourines, danced, and sang:

> Sing to the LORD, for he has triumphed gloriously;
> horse and rider he has thrown into the sea.
> Exod 15:21

Their action was the performance of bodily freedom, for their bodies had long ached with unbearable work. As I pondered their song and dance of freedom, I noted the contemporary parallel as the protestors danced in the streets in DC where the huge yellow letters spelled out "Black Lives Matter." It was as though the protestors sensed that they had, at least for now, escaped and moved beyond the coercive fear and greed of the predatory economy of U.S. patriarchal capitalism. That dance, like that earlier dance of Miriam, gave bodily articulation for bodies now permitted their full joyous freedom, even if under the all-seeing eye of Pharaoh's surveillance.

At the same time, however, a move beyond the reach and governance of Pharaoh meant that the erstwhile slaves could no longer count on the certitudes and predictabilities of Pharaoh; as a result, the wilderness felt like a free fall into risk. Without Pharaoh's jobs, how would they pay the rent? It is for that reason that as soon as the slaves crossed out of Exodus 15 and Egypt into Exodus 16 and the wilderness, in that moment they wished for a prompt return to Pharaoh, ready to trade their newly found freedom for the certitude of Pharaoh's bread supply:

> "If only we had died by the hand of the LORD in the land of Egypt, when we sat by the fleshpots and ate our fill of bread; for you have brought us out into this wilderness to kill this whole assembly with hunger."
>
> Exod 16:3

Our circumstance is like that now, as the loss of Pharaoh's jobs generates great risk. Under the ravages of the pandemic, the failures of Pharaoh's system have been revealed even more fully, and the people cry out for change. Yet wilderness can also evoke great soberness and a wish for return to the way it was "back there." The wilderness marked by great joy can readily enough turn to anxiety and nostalgia for the old security:

> "If only we had meat to eat! We remember the fish we used to eat in Egypt for nothing, the cucumbers, the melons, the leeks, the onions, and the garlic; but now our strength is dried up, and there is nothing at all but his manna to look at."
>
> Num 11:4–6

Some soon wearied of their new circumstance and wished for the regularities of the old system of coercion. I suppose the contemporary appeal to "law and order" is designed to call attention to the fact that *emancipation* for some feels like *anarchy* to others.

The wilderness is a new liminal environment that requires fresh constructive thinking and action. So now in the moment of emancipated bodies, the wilderness requires hard thinking and bold action for the sake of an alternative social apparatus. It is one thing to cross the water into freedom. It is quite another thing to morph from the dance of freedom to a viable shared life there. In the memory of ancient Israel, that is the burden of the wilderness-like moment of the later Babylonian exile when Israel finds itself in a new world now void of city, king, and temple:

> Build houses and live in them; plant gardens and eat what they produce. Take wives and have sons and daughters; take wives for your sons, and give your daughters in marriage, that they may bear sons and daughters; multiply there, and do not decrease.
>
> Jer 29:5–6

The prophetic tradition of Israel exhibits poetic-prophetic efforts at such imagination outside the sphere of the coercive regime of Jerusalem and beyond the reach of imperial Babylon, a stand-in for Pharaoh. Thus Isaiah can imagine a new alternative city (65:17–25). Jeremiah can evoke a new grace-laden covenant (31:31–34). And Ezekiel can sketch out a new symmetrical city with abiding holiness at its center (48:1–35). Actual social reality may take the form of none of these poetic offers, but the wilderness inhabitants cannot shortcut the imaginative efforts that run beyond anything thinkable or imaginable amid the coercion of Pharaoh. (It is for the same reason that Jesus told parables, acts of imagination beyond administered reality in the Roman Empire.) It is the work to be done after the first flush of dancing in order to be sure that there is no reembrace of Pharaoh, because Pharaoh, despite all hopes, has not and will not change. Pharaoh will continue to be coercive and predatory. Wilderness is the hard work of alternative!

II.

Pharaoh's monopoly of grain assured that there was in Egypt a steady supply of food. In contrast to Pharaoh's

Egypt, *the wilderness is a place without visible life-supports.* While the Israelites were eager to escape Egypt, they found the wilderness to be a place bereft of life's sustenance—bread, meat, water. It did not take long to discover that they faced, in the wilderness, a most precarious existence. Some promptly yearned for a return to Egypt. Even though they had known harsh oppression there, what they remembered about Egypt, rather than oppression, was a reliable food supply:

> "Why is the LORD bringing us into this land to fall by the sword? Our wives and our little ones will become booty; would it not be better for us to go back to Egypt?" So they said to one another, "Let us choose a captain, and go back to Egypt."
>
> Num 14:3–4

There was a sustained complaint against the leadership of Moses, for he was not able to guarantee a food supply in the way that Pharaoh had. The wilderness left the freed slaves with an option, so it seemed to them, of death or resubmission to Pharaoh's Egypt. Of course, it is like that amid the virus as we face an awareness that an income necessary for life can be had only with participation in the capitalist economic system. Thus the "reopening of the economy" can be seen, in some ways, as similar to a desire to return to Egypt, a readiness to risk the virus for the sake of livability. The capitalist system on which we are dependent seemingly leaves us with only this either/or choice.

In the wilderness material of the Bible, we are offered two narratives that attest that the wilderness, presided over by the generous creator God, does indeed contain viable life supports, even though they are not easily visible and even though they do not take conventional form.

In the more familiar account of Exodus 16, the complaint is against the leadership of Moses. Moses, however, deflects the complaint away from himself and onto YHWH (v. 7). In response to the complaint of Israel, it is remembered that YHWH heard the complaint and responded with great gifts of food. First there came quail to supply meat (v. 13). And then there was bread; it "was a fine flakey substance, as fine as frost on the ground" (v. 14). That gift of bread was not something they recognized. They asked about its identity: "What is it?" (*man hu'*) (v. 15). That question became the name of the new bread, so that *man hu'* morphed to *manna*. The peculiar name for the peculiar bread of the wilderness was the consequence of an unanswered wonderment. "What is it" is gift bread that escapes all conventional expectations and that defies all conventional explanations. The wonder of the bread is that wilderness turns into a place of ample bread!

> "Gather as much of it as each of you needs, an omer to a person according to the number of persons, all providing for those in their own tents." The Israelites did so, some gathering more, some less. But they measured it with an omer, those who gatherered much had nothing over, and those who gathered little had no shortage; they gathered as much as each of them needed.
>
> Exod 16:16–18

Divinely given abundance is the response to crisis complaint! That strange gift is amplified in the next chapter. Now there is no water, for wilderness is an arid place (17:2). Again there is complaint against the leadership of Moses. Again Moses deflects the complaint from himself to the Lord. Again the Lord responds in a way beyond expectation: "'Strike the rock, and water will come out of it, so that the people may drink'" (17:6). "Water from rock" is not unlike "blood from a turnip"! It turns out that the wilderness is a place of ample water. Thus Israel receives, beyond any explanation and outside the delivery system of Pharaoh, the necessities of meat, bread, and water. The wilderness where YHWH presides teems with viable life supports that become visible by the inscrutable gift of the God of abundance.

A second narrative reflects the same wilderness crisis. In Numbers 11, Israel is again desperate for food, this time fatigued with the manna that has become excessively familiar to them. This time, however, Moses refuses to be YHWH's advocate. He sides with the complaining Israelites against YHWH:

> "Why have you treated your servant so badly? Why have I not found favor in your sight, that you lay the burden of all this people on me? Did I conceive all this people? Did I give birth to them, that you should say to me, 'Carry them in your bosom, as a nurse carries a sucking child, to the land that you promised on oath to their ancestors'? Where am I to get meat to give to all this people? For they come weeping to me and say, 'Give us meat to eat!' I am not able to carry all this people alone, for they are too heavy for me. If this is the way you are going to treat me, put me to death at once—if I have found favor in your sight— and do not let me see my misery."
>
> Num 11:11–15

Moses has had more than enough of the responsibility in his impossible leadership role. He voices the sense that he has not received adequate backup from God. YHWH responds to Moses' desperate demand:

"Therefore the LORD will give you meat, and you shall eat. You shall eat not only one day, or two days, or five days, or ten days, or twenty days, but for a whole month—until it comes out of your nostrils and become loathsome to you—because you have rejected the LORD who is among you, and have wailed before him, saying, 'Why did we ever leave Egypt?'"

Num 11:18-20

That divine response is not generous and gracious. As Moses is fed up with Israel's complaints, so YHWH is fed up with the complaints of Israel and Moses. YHWH promises ample meat but makes the promise in a fit of anger so that the promised meat will be the cause of respiratory problems perhaps not unlike the virus. Indeed the threat of YHWH is strong enough that we might expect a desperate response from Israel with too many quail, "I can't breathe!" We may observe here that even in the midst of potential abundance, human experience is beset with the threat of contingency, whether traced to biological cause, human action, or some so-called act of God—intensified exponentially for those who suffer systemic discrimination. The narrative ends with an ample gift of quail that had been promised:

Then a wind went out from the LORD, and it brought quails from the sea and let them fall beside the camp, about a day's journey on this side and a day's journey on the other side, all around the camp, about two cubits deep on the ground. So the people worked all that day and night and all the next day, gathering the quails.

Num 11:31-32

It was a gift from God marked by divine anger that ended in strife and destruction.

It is not difficult to imagine a like outcome of the protests concerning police misconduct. One can imagine a *quail fight* among leaders with a delay in any real social gains. It turns out that the wilderness of protest is laden with gifts. But those gifts cannot be easily converted into any familiar social form. The food crisis in the wilderness required the articulation of newly imagined forms of common life. In this case the newly imagined form of Israel's common life is the Sabbath (Exod 16:22–26). The regular observance of Sabbath is acknowledgment that Israel is on the receiving end of life's sustenance. Israel does not possess or generate such sustenance but receives it as a gift. And when Israel subsequently defiles Sabbath for the sake of commerce, big trouble is sure to come (see Amos 8:4–6). Thus the generous food supply of the wilderness cannot be accommodated to the predatory practices of Pharaoh, for the food hoarded will melt, get worms, and smell badly (Exod 16:20–21). A failure of faithful imagination could cause Israel, from the wilderness, to replicate the economy and social practices of Pharaoh.

So now among us a failure of imagination might lead to a replication of the old forms of our common life that bring with them conventional practices of exploitation, predation, and abuse. It is not easy to maintain alternative in the practice of real-life economy. That, nevertheless, is the mandate of Moses and every community that wants to order life apart from Pharaoh's drama of oppression. The wilderness gifts of sustenance require "a more excellent way" (1 Cor 12:31). This immense challenge for those who refuse Pharaoh's way is to continue to imagine, invent, and devise transformative ways to be together in the world. Eventually the wilderness people arrive at Sinai. There they will receive ten mandates as alternative to Pharaoh (Exod 20:1–17). The mandates concern *the holiness of God*, which deabsolutizes everything else, and the *centrality of the neighbor*. It is clear from Sinai and thereafter that these mandates contradict Pharaoh, for Pharaoh defied the holiness of God and dismissed the centrality of the neighbor. Wilderness food comes with built-in requirements. The challenge for Israel was to move out of wilderness into the land of promise and there to continue the disciplines of wilderness in the midst of storable crops:

> The manna ceased on the day they ate the produce of the land, and the Israelites no longer had manna; they ate the crops of the land of Canaan that year.
>
> Josh 5:12

The challenge now is to practice *manna-life* in an environment of guaranteed harvest crops. As Scott has shown in his history of state formation, *Against the Grain*, the capacity to store grain (or other kinds of commodity wealth) can readily lead to *storage, surplus*, and concomitant *subsistence*, as well as the violence necessary to maintain the unequal interface. When the memory of wilderness fades and wilderness trust and gratitude are not urgent, the prospect for genuine social alternative readily descends into the "same old, same old."

III.

Pharaoh kept a tight lid on protest and complaint. No complaint in the brickyard . . . or in the meat-packing job . . . or in prison . . . or in a nursing home! Pharaoh requires that we simply suck it up and keep moving, whereby our silence offers tacit assent to the rule of Pharaoh. But, of course, the censoring of protest and complaint can last only so long. Eventually all hell will break loose: "After a long time the king of Egypt died. The Israelites groaned under their slavery, and cried out" (Exod 2:23). When their grievance breaks loose, there is no limit to its scope and no limit to the danger such loudness poses for oppressive power.

It is not surprising that when Israel arrived in the wilderness it was completely prepared to "murmur." It is clear that *the wilderness is a venue for loud, legitimate protest in anger, impatience, demand, and hope.* Of course, much of the protest in the wilderness is a response to present circumstance in the wilderness, with a scarcity of meat, bread, and water. But we may imagine as well, however, that the protest of murmuring is more vigorous because of the long silencing imposed by Pharaoh. It is as though Israel in the wilderness, like a young child, has just learned a new sound of her voice and is sure to use it repeatedly. The wilderness is a place that evokes, permits, and hosts loud protests that make demands we had been taught by Pharaoh to deny. For that reason, the wilderness narrative is filled with persistent protest:

> And the people *complained* against Moses, saying, "What shall we drink?"
>
> Exod 15:24

> "In the morning you shall see the glory of the LORD, because he has heard your *complaining* against the LORD. For what are we, that you *complain* against us?" And Moses said, "When the LORD gives you meat to eat in the evening and your fill of bread in the morning, because the LORD has heard the *complaining* that you utter against him—what are we? Your *complaining* is not against us but against the LORD."
>
> Exod 16:7–8

> But the people thirsted there for water; and the people *complained* against Moses and said, "Why did

you bring us out of Egypt, to kill us and our children and livestock with thirst?"

Exod 17:3

How long shall this wicked congregation *complain* against me? I have heard the complaints of the Israelites, which they *complain* against me. . . . Your dead bodies shall fall in this very wilderness; and of all your number, included in the census . . . who have *complained* against me.

Num 14:27, 29

They are an unhappy bunch in the wilderness!

The wonder of the narrative is that the complaints are heard, taken seriously, and given a response. Thus Israel's protests are variously answered by God with meat, bread, and water. It turns out that the wilderness is a place of heavy-duty dialogic engagement in which the One with authority is attentive to and responsive to the needs and requirements of the vulnerable ones. This engagement between *authority* and *vulnerability* is an astonishing reality in the wilderness. This is so unlike Pharaoh in Egypt, who in hard-heartedness never heard a complaint and in harshness dismissed any voicing of groan from below.

In our season of wilderness reality with the coronavirus, the economic crisis, and the pandemic of police misconduct, it is remarkable that we have arrived at vigorous, out-loud protest. All sorts of people have been finding their voice; all sorts of people are hoping and insisting in solidarity with those who face the ominous realities of repression, brutality, and abandonment. This out-loud self-declaration from below is a new social reality among us. There can be no more top-down silencing of the kind that Pharaoh perfected. It remains to be seen whether top-down civic authority can recognize this wilderness moment with a readiness for serious dialogic engagement, or whether we may expect more Pharonic silencing and abdication. In the wilderness narrative, we get a fresh glimpse of God who now is known to be the one who can be effectively engaged "from below." It may be that we will get a new glimpse of social power among us, power that can effectively respond to out-loud self-announcement. The wilderness is not and cannot be a place of silence or silencing. It is rather a venue for protest, for acknowledged need, and for hope. The protesters around us have not acted out of cynicism or despair; they have acted in hope of transformative outcomes, just as Israel in the wilderness hoped for newness from the God to whom they protested.

Eventually the people of promise arrived at the land of promise. But the journey there is wilderness-laden. It remains to be seen whether in our time and place we will have the stamina and courage for a wilderness-laden enterprise of insistent hope. The wonder of wilderness is that there the erstwhile slaves encountered a God willing and able to engage with them, all so unlike their life with Pharaoh!

The faith of a wilderness people has entered Christian liturgy in the familiar hymn of William Williams:

> Guide me, O thou great Jehovah,
> pilgrim through this barren land.
> I am weak, but thou art mighty.
> Hold me with thy powerful hand.
> Bread of heaven, bread of heaven,
> feed me till I want no more;
> feed me till I want no more.
>
> Open now the crystal fountain,
> whence the healing stream doth flow.
> Let the fire and cloudy pillar

> lead me all my journey through.
> Strong deliverer, strong deliverer,
> be thou still my strength and shield;
> be thou still my strength and shield.
>
> When I tread the verge of Jordan,
> bid my anxious fears subside.
> Death of death, and hell's destruction,
> land me safe on Canaan's side.
> Songs of praises, songs of praises
> I will ever give to thee;
> I will ever give to thee.[2]

The hymn acknowledges a wilderness condition of weakness and vulnerability; that weakness and vulnerability, of course, are countered by trusting affirmation in the might, power, and fidelity of the God who governs the wilderness. It is this God who will give bread.

The second stanza imagines the reliable guidance of God in places of risk and exposure by "fire and cloudy pillar," never doubting that God is present and reliable (see Exod 13:21). The third stanza features arrival at the place and land of promise marked by the boundary of the Jordan River. Thus the hymn echoes the cadences of hope and food, of risk and confidence, of threat and arrival. We are now in such a wilderness time when the old certitudes of Pharaoh are exposed as false, but when the arrival in a new place of well-being is only an anticipation. We are in between; that, of course, is where faith has a chance to make a decisive difference, if we can be confident that the God of faithfulness gives new goodness. It is a conviction verified in the wilderness sojourn of Jesus. He was tempted when

2. William Williams, "Guide Me, O Thou Great Jehovah," *Glory to God* (Louisville, KY: Westminster John Knox Press, 2013), 65.

the force of evil tried to talk him out of his vocation. Then we are told: "Suddenly angels came and waited on him" (Matt 4:11). It turns out that the wilderness, contrary to our fear and our conventional expectations, is securely governed by God who dispatches angels of mercy at points of need among the faithful. While it may take Pharaoh time to realize it, we have, in our society, departed Egypt. We are not yet at a new place of well-being. We are in between, making the risky journey in faith. Within these next chapters, I attempt to provide something of a map for this risky way:

- I will consider the *Exodus* narrative as the account of the journey now required of the faithful in the move from a culture of anxiety to a practice of neighborliness.
- I will consider the *Jeremiah* oracle as an invitation to a radical choice for life or for death.
- I will consider the *Isaiah* sequence of texts as a reliable script for contemporary practice of loss and restoration in a failed urban economy.

In my judgment, these texts will summon and engage and reassure the church on this demanding way, assisting in its missional stance to faithfully resist hegemonic ideologies that suck the life out of our socioeconomic neighborhoods. I have no doubt that when such an interpretive exercise in contemporaneity is led by the Spirit, it will make a difference for that church and for those the church is responsible to. Being on the way, as we are, is hazardous. That risky way, however, is fully within the governing orbit of the faithful God. That conviction gives us courage to depart Pharaoh, readiness to receive new gifts that we cannot see, and freedom for loud articulation of hope-filled hurt and grief.

Walter Brueggemann
June 11, 2020

Chapter 1

THE JOURNEY TO THE COMMON GOOD

Faith, Anxiety, and the Practice of Neighborliness

The great crisis among us is the crisis of "the common good," the sense of community solidarity that binds all in a common destiny—haves and have-nots, the rich and the poor. We face a crisis about the common good because there are powerful forces at work among us to resist the common good, to violate community solidarity, and to deny a common destiny. Mature people, at their best, are people who are committed to the common good that reaches beyond private interest, transcends sectarian commitments, and offers human solidarity.

In my comments, I will consider texts from the Hebrew Scriptures/Old Testament that may inform our thinking about the common good. This concern is not an easy or obvious one, because clearly the Hebrew Bible/ Old Testament is permeated with impediments to the common good, including the pervasive influence of patriarchy, ethnicity, race, sect, and party, not even to mention the layers of human and divine anger that pervade its pages.[1] Nonetheless, the issue of common good arises in its pages precisely because the Hebrew Bible/Old Testament is the

---

1. For the deep problematic of the claims for God in the Old Testament, see Regina M. Schwartz, *The Curse of Cain: The Violent Legacy of Monotheism* (Chicago: University of Chicago Press, 1997); and Marvin A. Sweeney, *Reading the Hebrew Bible after the Shoah: Engaging Holocaust Theology* (Minneapolis: Fortress Press, 2008).

1

oldest text we have in the West that claims to be revelatory of truth out beyond us.

So I begin this way:

- The journey to the common good in this text is *a memory* of the way in which ancient Israel moved from Pharaoh's slave labor arrangements to the holy mountain of covenanting at Sinai.
- That journey, deeply remembered in ancient Israel, became the script and the itinerary that *Jews*, over many generations, have made, always again from Egyptian exploitation to the holy mountain. The Jews make that journey, in liturgical imagination, over and over again, most visibly in the imaginative enterprise of Passover.
- *Christians*, in a derivative way, make that journey alongside Jews, rooted in the same ancient memory. Christians do so in the company of Jews, though of course we Christians are frequently tempted to imagine that the script belongs to us and not to Jews.
- Jews, and along with them Christians, make an offer and issue an invitation to *wider humanity* to join the journey, because that hard trek is required not only by the particular passions of Jewishness or of Christian sensibility. Rather, the journey to the common good is a trek that all serious human beings must make, a growth out beyond private interest and sectarian passion.

I will exposit that journey as it is remembered from ancient Israel. I will treat it as a historical memory; as I do so, I will be aware that in various contexts the memory is a present literary-liturgical construction given voice by Jews, by

Christians, and by others who may be fellow travelers with Jews and Christians. The textual memory to which I appeal has great porous openness to other renderings, as long as those renderings remain attentive to the story line. I articulate that defining journey in three moments.

I

Israel begins its core memory in the grip of Pharaoh's Egypt. Indeed, we may take ancient Pharaoh (as a cipher and metaphor in the Hebrew Bible/Old Testament) as the paradigmatic enemy of the common good, an agent of immense power who could not get beyond his acquisitive interest to ponder the common good. Pharaoh is an example and an embodiment of a complex system of monopoly that, along with the wealth that it produces, inflicts anxiety that affects every dimension of the system:

1. Pharaoh's Egypt is the breadbasket of the ancient world. Already in Genesis 12, the very first chapter of Israel in the Old Testament, we learn that Pharaoh had ample food and could supply the entire world:

> Now there was a famine in the land. So Abram went down to Egypt to reside there as an alien, for the famine was severe in the land.
>
> Gen 12:10

It was natural and automatic that the Nile Valley should produce bread. A need for bread drove Abraham to the place of security and sufficiency.

2. There is high irony in the report that Pharaoh, the leader of the superpower, has bad dreams. He might

be competent and in control all day long, but when he is asleep at night and his guard is down and his competence is relaxed, he has nightmares. The one with everything has dreams of insecurity:

> Then Pharaoh said to Joseph, "In my dream I was standing on the banks of the Nile; and seven cows, fat and sleek, came up out of the Nile and fed in the reed grass. Then seven other cows came up after them, poor, very ugly, and thin. Never had I seen such ugly ones in all the land of Egypt. The thin and ugly cows ate up the first seven fat cows, but when they had eaten them no one would have known that they had done so, for they were still as ugly as before. Then I awoke. I fell asleep a second time and I saw in my dream seven ears of grain, full and good, growing on one stalk, and seven ears, withered, thin, and blighted by the east wind, sprouting after them; and the thin ears swallowed up the seven good ears."
>
> Gen 41:17–24

He is desperate to find out the meaning of the dream; but no one in the intelligence community of his empire can decode the secret message.

Finally, as a last resort, he summons an unknown Israelite from prison. According to this ancient narrative, the uncredentialed Israelite can decode what the empire cannot discern. Joseph the interpreter immediately grasps the point. The nightmare is about *scarcity*. The one with everything dreams of *deficiency*. The cows and the shocks of grain anticipate years of famine when no food will be produced.

3. Pharaoh receives the interpretation of his nightmare and sets about to make imperial policy. As readers of the narrative, we are permitted to watch while the *nightmare* is turned into *policy*. Pharaoh asks for a plan of action, and Joseph, modest man that he is, nominates himself as food czar:

> Now therefore let Pharaoh select a man who is discerning and wise, and set him over the land of Egypt.
>
> Gen 41:33

Joseph, blessed Israelite that he is, is not only a shrewd dream interpreter; he is, as well, an able administrator who commits himself to Pharaoh's food policy. The royal policy is to accomplish a food monopoly. In that ancient world as in any contemporary world, food is a weapon and a tool of control.

We learn of *policy* rooted in *nightmare* (Gen 47:13-26). The peasants, having no food of their own, come to Joseph, now a high-ranking Egyptian, and pay their money in exchange for food so that the centralized government of Pharaoh achieves even greater wealth (v. 14). After the money is all taken, the peasants come again and ask for food. This time Joseph, on behalf of Pharaoh, takes their cattle, what Karl Marx would have termed their "means of production" (vv. 15-17). In the next year, the third year, the peasants still need food. But they have no money and they have no livestock. In the third year, they gladly surrender their freedom in exchange for food:

Shall we die before your eyes, both we and our land? Buy us and our land in exchange for food. We with our land will become slaves to Pharaoh; just give us seed, so that we may live and not die, and that the land may not become desolate.

Gen 47:19

And the inevitable outcome:

So Joseph bought all the land of Egypt for Pharaoh. All the Egyptians sold their fields, because the famine was severe upon them; and the land became Pharaoh's. As for the people, he made slaves of them from one end of Egypt to the other.

Gen 47:20–21

Slavery in the Old Testament happens because the strong ones work a monopoly over the weak ones and eventually exercise control over their bodies. Not only that, but in the end, the peasants, now become slaves, are grateful for their dependent status:

They said, "You have saved our lives; may it please my lord, we will be slaves to Pharaoh."

Gen 47:25

This is an ominous tale filled with irony, a part of the biblical text we do not often enough note. We know about the exodus deliverance, but we do not take notice that slavery occurred by the manipulation of the economy in the interest of a concentration of wealth and power for the few at the expense of the community. In reading the Joseph narrative, we characteristically focus on the providential texts of Genesis 45:1–15 and 50:20, to the neglect of the down-and-dirty narratives of economic transaction.

With reference to the common good, we may formulate a tentative conclusion about the narrative of Pharaoh: *Those who are living in anxiety and fear, most especially fear of scarcity, have no time or energy for the common good.* Anxiety is no adequate basis for the common good; anxiety will cause the formulation of policy and of exploitative practices that are inimical to the common good, a systemic greediness that precludes the common good. Fear-driven nationalism is a poor beginning point for policy!

II

By the end of the book of Genesis, we have a deteriorated social situation consisting in Pharaoh and the state slaves who submit their bodies to slavery in order to receive food from the state monopoly. All parties in this arrangement are beset by anxiety, the slaves because they are exploited, Pharaoh because he is fearful and on guard. The narrative of the book of Exodus is organized into a great contest that is, politically and theologically, an exhibit of the ongoing contest between the *urge to control* and the *power of emancipation* that in ancient Israel is perennially linked to the God of the exodus.

We are given a picture of the frantic, aggressive policies of the empire that are propelled by anxiety:

1. In Exodus 5, we learn that the imperial system is a system of raw and ruthless exploitation, always pressing cheap labor for more production. Chapter 5 of the book of Exodus is permeated with harsh pharaonic commands to the cheap labor force, unbearable labor conditions, and unrealistic production schedules:

But the king of Egypt said to them, "Moses and Aaron, why are you taking the people away from their work? Get to your labors!"

Exod 5:4

That same day Pharaoh commanded the taskmasters of the people, as well as their supervisors, "You shall no longer give the people straw to make bricks, as before; let them go and gather straw for themselves. But you shall require of them the same quantity of bricks as they have made previously; do not diminish it, for they are lazy; that is why they cry, 'Let us go and offer sacrifice to our God.' Let heavier work be laid on them; then they will labor at it and pay no attention to deceptive words."

Exod 5:6–9

The supervisors simply carry out the demands of the empire:

So the taskmasters and the supervisors of the people went out and said to the people, "Thus says Pharaoh, 'I will not give you straw. Go and get straw yourselves, wherever you can find it; but your work will not be lessened in the least.' "

Exod 5:10–11

The taskmasters are relentless:

The taskmasters were urgent, saying, "Complete your work, the same daily assignment as when you were given straw." And the supervisors of the Israelites, whom Pharaoh's taskmasters had set over them, were beaten, and were asked, "Why did you not finish the required quantity of bricks yesterday and today, as you did before?"

Exod 5:13–14

The production schedule, propelled by the king with the bad dreams, assumes that production that will enhance centralized authority is the purpose of all labor.

2. The aggressive policies of Pharaoh have a purpose other than mere exploitation. The narrative shows that Pharaoh is scared to death of his own workforce. He fears their departure, the loss of labor, and the humiliation of the empire. In his fear, Pharaoh becomes even more abrasive:

The Egyptians became ruthless in imposing tasks on the Israelites, and made their lives bitter with hard service in mortar and brick and in every kind of field labor. They were ruthless in all the tasks that they imposed on them.

Exod 1:13–14

The resounding word *ruthless* bespeaks an exploitative system that no longer thinks well about productivity. The fear that lies behind such policy finally leads to an assault on the labor force that provides for the killing of all baby boys that are potentially part of the workforce:

When you act as midwives to the Hebrew women, and see them on the birthstool, if it is a boy, kill him; but if it is a girl, she shall live.

Exod 1:16

The insanity of the policy is that Pharaoh now destroys precisely those who would be the next generation of workers.

3. The move from economic exploitation to policies that are grounded in fear seems deliberately designed to produce suffering. Finally, as every exploitative system eventually learns, the exploitation rooted in fear reaches its limit of unbearable suffering. Two things happen:

First, the unbearable suffering comes to public speech. Totalitarian regimes seek to keep suffering silent and invisible for as long as possible. But finally, as every totalitarian regime eventually learns, human suffering will not stay silent. There is a cry! It is the irreducible human reality of suffering that must have voice. It is only a cry, an articulation of raw bodily dismay. That is as close as we come in this narrative to prayer. Prayer here is truth—the truth of bodily pain—sounding its inchoate demand. The cry is not addressed to anyone. It is simply out there, declaring publicly that the social system of the empire has failed.

But second, as the biblical narrative has it—most remarkably—the cry of abused labor found its way to the ears of YHWH who, in this narrative, is reckoned to be a central player in the public drama of social power. The cry is not addressed to YHWH; but it comes to YHWH because YHWH is a magnet that draws the cries of the abused:[2]

Out of the slavery their cry for help rose up to God. God heard their groaning, and God remembered his covenant with Abraham, Isaac, and Jacob. God

2. See James Kugel, *The God of Old: Inside the Lost World of the Bible* (New York: Free Press, 2003), chapter 5, on the linkage between the human cry and the propensity of the God of the Bible.

looked upon the Israelites, and God took notice of them.

Exod 2:23b–25

The human cry, so the Bible asserts, evokes divine resolve. There is a divine resolve to transform the economic situation of the slaves. It is, at the same time, inescapably, a divine resolve to delegitimate Pharaoh and to wrest social initiative away from the empire.

4. The practice of exploitation, fear, and suffering produces a decisive moment in human history. This dramatic turn away from aggressive centralized power and a food monopoly features a fresh divine resolve for an alternative possibility, a resolve that in turn features raw human agency. The biblical narrative is very careful and precise about how it transposes *divine resolve* into *human agency*. That transposition is declared in the encounter of the burning bush wherein Moses is addressed and summoned by this self-declaring God. The outcome of that inscrutable mystery of encounter is that Moses is invested with the vision of the slave community in its departure from the imperial economy. The words that go with the encounter are words of *divine resolve:*

> Then the LORD said, "I have observed the misery of my people who are in Egypt; I have heard their cry on account of their taskmasters. Indeed, I know their sufferings, and I have come down to deliver them from the Egyptians, and to bring them up out of that land to a good and broad land, a land flowing with milk and honey, to the country of the Canaanites, the Hittites, the Amorites, the Perizzites, the Hivites, and the Jebusites. The cry of the Israelites has

now come to me; I have also seen how the Egyptians oppress them."

Exod 3:7–9

But the divine resolve turns abruptly to *human agency* in verse 10:

So come, I will send you to Pharaoh to bring my people, the Israelites, out of Egypt.

The outcome is a human agent who can act and dream outside imperial reality. And dreaming outside imperial reality, that human agent can begin the daring extrication of this people from the imperial system.

There is, surely, some high irony in the juxtaposition of Pharaoh and Moses. Pharaoh is a dreamer, but he dreams only of the nightmare of scarcity. But contrast Moses, who, after the burning bush, can indeed say, "I have a dream."

I have a dream of departure,
I have a dream beyond brick quotas,
I have a dream beyond the regime of exploitation
    and fear,
I have a dream outside the zone of strategically
    designed suffering.

The dream of Moses sharply contrasts with the nightmare of Pharaoh. It is that dream that propels the biblical narrative. Pharaoh and Moses, along with all of his people, had been contained in a system of anxiety. There was enough anxiety for everyone, but there was not and could not be a common good. The anxiety system of Pharaoh precluded the common good. The imperial arrangement made everyone into a master or a slave, a threat or an accomplice, a rival or a slave. For the sake of the common good, it was necessary to depart *the anxiety system* that produces *nightmares of scarcity*.

III

They did depart! In Exodus 14, the slaves watched the waters open for them (vv. 21–23). In Exodus 15, they were across the waters, outside the system, where they looked back and danced and sang and praised YHWH, who had delivered them. And by Exodus 16, they are underway on the long trek to well-being. In chapter 16, they take their first generative steps out into the wilderness—the wilderness is where one ends up if one departs the anxiety system of Pharaoh.

The slaves departed the anxiety system; but by verse 3 of chapter 16, deep in the wilderness, they began to complain about their new environment of risky faith; they yearned to resubmit to the anxious exploitation of Pharaoh:

> The Israelites said to them, "If only we had died by the hand of the LORD in the land of Egypt, when we sat by the fleshpots and ate our fill of bread; for you have brought us out into this wilderness to kill this whole assembly with hunger."
>
> Exod 16:3

They remembered slavery as a place of guaranteed food. Later they would recall their slave diet with some relish:

> The rabble among them had a strong craving; and the Israelites also wept again, and said, "If only we

had meat to eat! We remember the fish we used to eat in Egypt for nothing, the cucumbers, the melons, the leeks, the onions, and the garlic; but now our strength is dried up, and there is nothing at all but this manna to look at."

Num 11:4–6

Their endless complaint mobilized Moses, who in turn complained to God, and God responded to the complaint; perhaps the divine response was a necessity because now YHWH, and not Pharaoh, is responsible for this people. YHWH issues an assurance:

I have heard the complaining of the Israelites; say to them, "At twilight you shall eat meat, and in the morning you shall have your fill of bread; then you shall know that I am the LORD your God."

Exod 16:12

The meat will be quail, and that came as promised. And concerning bread in the morning, the narrative reports:

When the layer of dew lifted, there on the surface of the wilderness was a fine flaky substance, as fine as frost on the ground.

Exod 16:14

The "bread of heaven" was like nothing they knew, and so they said to one another, as they watched the gift of bread fall on them, "What is it?" The Hebrew for that question is *man hu'*, and so the bread is called "manna." The bread is named "What is it?" which makes it a "wonder bread" that fit none of their prevailing categories; they wondered what it was.

Now it takes little imagination to see that this narrative of bread in the wilderness is a very different sort of narrative contrasted with that of the exodus. The exodus narrative is credible and realistic, all about exploited cheap labor and escape from an impossible production schedule. Compared with that, this narrative of bread from heaven is a dreamy narrative that lacks that kind of realism. But then, consider that there is something inescapably dreamy and unreal about inexplicable generosity. When we hear of it, we wonder about it and doubt it, because it does not fit our expectations for a quid pro quo world. Indeed, about such divine generosity there is something so dreamy that we reserve for it the special term *miracle*, something outside the ordinary, something that breaks the pattern of the regular and the expected, something that violates the predictable. So consider this sequence of great words, "dreamy, inexplicable, generous, miracle." Finally we will come to the word *grace*, a reach of divine generosity not based on the recipient but on the giver. If we juxtapose the words *grace* and *wilderness*, we come to the claim of this narrative of wonder bread. "Wilderness" is a place, in biblical rhetoric, where there are no viable life support systems. "Grace" is the occupying generosity of God that redefines the place. The wonder bread, as a gesture of divine grace, recharacterizes the wilderness that Israel now discovered to be a place of viable life, made viable by the generous inclination of YHWH.

If we pursue this juxtaposition of "grace" and "wilderness," later we will find it explicit in the poetry of the prophet Jeremiah. That prophet uses the word *wilderness* to refer to the sixth-century exile, a subsequent locus for the life of Israel that also lacked viable life supports. In that

locus of death, Israel found sustaining divine presence so
that the prophet can say of God's miracle:

> Thus says the LORD:
> The people who survived the sword
>   found *grace* in the *wilderness;*
> when Israel sought for rest,
>   the LORD appeared to him from far away.
>
> Jer 31:2–3a

It is impossible to overstate the significance of "grace in the
wilderness," given in the palpable form of bread that could
sustain in an unsustainable context. That moment of wonder, awe, and generosity, in an instant, radically redefined
the place in which Israel now had to live in its new freedom,
outside the zone of imperial anxiety.

So, the narrative tells us, the bread in the wilderness
was a divine gesture of enormous abundance:

> Moses said to them, "It is the bread that the LORD
> has given you to eat. This is what the LORD has com-
> manded: 'Gather as much of it as each of you needs,
> an omer to a person according to the number of per-
> sons, all providing for those in their own tents.'"
> The Israelites did so, some gathering more, some
> less. But when they measured it with an omer, those
> who gathered much had nothing over, and those
> who gathered little had no shortage; they gathered as
> much as each of them needed.
>
> Exod 16:15–18

This narrative stands at the center of Israel's imagination;
it embodies and signifies YHWH's *capacity for generosity*

that stands in complete contrast to the *nightmare of scarcity* that fueled Pharaoh's rapacious policies. The Israelites were so inured to the scarcity system of Pharaoh that they could hardly take in the alternative abundance given in divine generosity, the purpose of which was to break the vicious cycle of anxiety about scarcity that in turn produced anger, fear, aggression, and, finally, predatory violence.

The Israelites, in the narrative, are overwhelmed by divine abundance. They react, however, as though they were still in the old system of pharaonic scarcity. Moses warned them not to save up or to hoard the bread or to keep extra supplies on hand:

> And Moses said to them, "Let no one leave any of it over until morning."
>
> Exod 16:19

Take what you need, eat and enjoy! But they did not listen. They filled their pockets and their baskets with extras because there might not be any more tomorrow. That is what one does in the face of scarcity. (It calls to mind the early days of the pandemic, when grocery shelves rapidly emptied as we stored up for another day when things might become even more scarce.)

But such frantic surpluses will not work. Because the "bread of heaven" is not like the "bread of affliction" that the Israelites had eaten in Egyptian slavery. There you could save a crust of bread for the next day. But not here! Abundance is not for hoarding. So, we are told:

> They did not listen to Moses; some left part of it until morning, and it *bred worms* and *became foul*. And

Moses was angry with them. Morning by morning they gathered it, as much as each needed; but when the sun grew hot, it *melted*.

Exod 16:20–21

The stored-up bread *bred worms*. It *smelled bad*. It *melted*. It would not last. Wonder bread lacks preservatives, because it is given daily, enough but not more, enough so that none need hunger. The bread of heaven is a contradiction to the rat race of production; the creator God who presides over the bread supply breaks the grip of Pharaoh's food monopoly; food is freely given outside the economic system that functions like an Egyptian pyramid with only a few on top of the heap.[3]

It is for good reason that in the Bible "bread" is the recurring sign of divine generosity, because it is the concrete indispensable resource for life in the world. In the narrative of the prophet Elisha, among the wonder men in ancient Israel, the narratives are often about bread:

- In 2 Kings 4:1–7, there is the abundant gift of oil given by the prophet so that the widow can pay her debts and prepare bread for the future.
- In 2 Kings 4:42–44, the same prophet has a limited supply of bread. But he feeds one hundred people and "has some left." The narrative attests that where the carriers of God's truth are at work, abundance overrides the scarcity of hunger.
- In 2 Kings 6:22–23, in the midst of Israel's perpetual war with Syria, the same prophet intervenes. The

---

3. For a reference to Egypt's pyramids in an analysis of political/economic trade-offs, see Peter L. Berger, *Pyramids of Sacrifice* (New York: Basic Books, 1975).

king of Israel wants to kill his Syrian prisoners of war, but the prophet will not permit it. Instead of death to the enemies, the prophet commands:

> Set food and water before them so that they may eat and drink; and let them go to their master.
>
> 2 Kgs 6:22

And the outcome of the generous meal:

> So he prepared for them a great feast; after they ate and drank, he sent them on their way, and they went to their master. And the Arameans no longer came raiding into the land of Israel.
>
> 2 Kgs 6:23

A "great feast" breaks the pattern of violence that is rooted in a fear of scarcity. The narrative attests that the world is not as we had imagined it, not as Pharaoh had organized it. Adherence to patterns of scarcity produces a world in which the generosity of God is nullified. The narratives attest otherwise and invite the listening community into an alternative mode of existence, one that is ordered according to divine generosity.

It is not different later in the poetry of Isaiah. In Isaiah 55, it is clear that the displaced Jews had fallen into the trap of the imperial system of Babylon. They had been carried away into the empire. For Jews with a long memory, being carried to Babylon was like being taken back to Pharaoh's Egypt, because all empires act the same way. All empires act according to the principle of scarcity, imagining that they need more land, more tax money, more revenue, more oil, more cheap labor, more energy. Some Jews had signed on for the new scarcity system that was just like the old scarcity system, once again inured to imperial expectation that left them frazzled and exhausted and cynical, because empires set quotas that can never be met.

In the midst of that new, unbearable context of scarcity, a context shaped not by facts on the ground but by ideological force, the prophet interrupts with an assertion and a question that raises hard issues about imperial ideology:

> Ho, everyone who thirsts,
>   come to the waters;
> and you that have no money,
>   come, buy and eat!
> Come, buy wine and milk
>   without money and without price.
>   Isa 55:1

Free food, free water, free milk, free wine—more than enough. The old divine gift of abundance in the wilderness is now renewed as abundance in exile. Then the question, which in fact is an accusation:

> Why do you spend your money for that which is not
>   bread,
>   and your labor for that which does not satisfy?
> Listen carefully to me, and eat what is good,
>   and delight yourselves in rich food.
>   Isa 55:2

The question is to Israelites, people of faith, who have succumbed to the scarcity system of Babylon, who have joined the rat race, and who have imagined that they could get ahead if they hustled more. The poet asks why they do that: "Why do you sign on for scarcity when you know the truth of God's abundance?"

Then comes a summons that follows from the *assurance of generosity* and the *question about the present scarcity:*

> Seek the LORD while he may be found,
>   call upon him while he is near;
> let the wicked forsake their way,
>   and the unrighteous their thoughts;
> let them return to the LORD, that he may have mercy
>   on them,
>   and to our God, for he will abundantly pardon.
>
> Isa 55:6–7

In specific location, this text is not a generic concern for sin and salvation. It is, rather, a summons away from the *scarcity system* to the *truth of generosity.* In location, the text is a summons to be a Jew with memories of abundance and a call to disengage from the ideology of scarcity that propels the empire. The poet knows that unless this summons is heeded, his listeners will remain perpetually unsatisfied, because the imperial pursuit of "more" can never be satisfied. Pharaoh can never have enough to sleep well at night. Pharaoh's ideology of anxiety will impinge on sleep even as it defines the economy. Both sleep and the economy remain restless!

What Israel discovered in the wilderness—and again in the exile—is that there is an alternative. Indeed, it is fair to say that the long history of Israel is a contestation between *Pharaoh's system of paucity* and *God's offer of abundance.* Surely it is a legitimate extrapolation that the long history of the church is a contest between *paucity* that presses to control and *abundance* that evokes patterns of generosity. Beyond Israel or church, going all the way back to Erik Erikson's elemental "basic trust," the human enterprise is a contrast between scarcity and the dreaminess of abundance that breaks the compulsions of scarcity.[4] Israel, full of wonder bread, makes its way to Mount Sinai. That gift of wonder *bread* as a miracle of *abundance* is a show of *generosity* that breaks the deathly pattern of anxiety, fear, greed, and anger, *a miracle* that always surprises because it is beyond our categories of expectation. It is precisely an overwhelming, inexplicable act of generosity that breaks the grip of self-destructive anxiety concerning scarcity.

IV

So they came to Sinai. They came from the *nightmare of paucity* by way of the *miracle of abundance*. What they discovered, as they approached the dread mountain of covenant, is that the gift of shalom had freed them from pharaonic scarcity so that they could have energy for the common good. They discovered at Mount Sinai that they could give energy to the neighborhood because the grip of *scarcity* had been broken by God's *abundance*. As they approached the mountain, long before they had heard any of God's commandments, they asserted, already in Exodus 19:8,

> The people all answered as one: "Everything that the LORD has spoken we will do."

4. Erik Erikson, *Identity and the Life Cycle: Selected Papers* (New York: International Universities Press, 1959), 55–65.

Israel signed on for a new obedience even before they had heard any of the commandments! The reason they did so is that they knew that any new commands from the God of abundance would be better than the commands of Pharaoh. The new commands at Sinai voiced YHWH's dream of a neighborhood, YHWH's intention for the common good. There was no common good in Egypt, because people in a scarcity system cannot entertain the common good.

This narrative from *anxiety* through *abundance* to *neighborhood* invites us to rethink the intention of the Ten Commandments. They are not rules for deep moralism. They are not commonsense rules designed to clobber and scold people. Rather, they are the most elemental statement of how to organize social power and social goods for the common benefit of the community. They are indeed "a new commandment" that is quite in contrast to the old commandments of Pharaoh:

- From commandments 1–3, Israel learned that YHWH is to be loved, served, and trusted rather than Pharaoh's security system:

    I am the LORD your God, who brought you out of the land of Egypt, out of the house of slavery; you shall have no other gods before me.

    You shall not make for yourself an idol, whether in the form of anything that is in heaven above, or that is on the earth beneath, or that is in the water under the earth. You shall not bow down to them or worship them; for I the LORD your God am a jealous God, punishing children for the iniquity of parents, to the third and the fourth generation of those who reject me, but showing steadfast love to

the thousandth generation of those who love me
and keep my commandments.

You shall not make wrongful use of the name of
the LORD your God, for the LORD will not acquit
anyone who misuses his name.

Exod 20:2–7

These three commandments are nothing less than regime
change; they declare that there is an alternative to the
anxiety-producing enterprise of Pharaoh. The command
is to worship the one who liberates from Pharaoh and to
honor the inscrutable holiness of the God who will not be
squeezed into any production system.

- Israel learned, from commandments 5–9, that neighbors, all kinds of neighbors, are to be respected and
  protected and not exploited:

Honor your father and your mother, so that
your days may be long in the land that the LORD
your God is giving you.

You shall not murder.

You shall not commit adultery.

You shall not steal.

You shall not bear false witness against your
neighbor.

Exod 20:12–16

These terse rules set a boundary on the way in which the
neighbor can be "used." Pharaoh, of course, knew no such
boundaries but was free to manage and manipulate neighbors in any way at all, in order to increase production. At
Sinai it is clear that neighbors are ends and not means,

agents in their own history and not merely cogs in a security system.

- Israel learned, from the tenth commandment, that there is a limit to acquisitiveness:

> You shall not covet your neighbor's house; you shall not covet your neighbor's wife, or male or female slave, or ox, or donkey, or anything that belongs to your neighbor.
>
> Exod 20:17

The commandment is not about petty acts of envy. It is about predatory practices and aggressive policies that make the little ones vulnerable to the ambitions of the big ones. In a rapacious economic system, nobody's house and nobody's field and nobody's wife and nobody's oil are safe from a stronger force. The exploitative system of Pharaoh believed that it always needed more and was always entitled to more—more bricks, more control, more territory, more oil—until it had everything. But, of course, one cannot order a neighborhood that way, because such practices and such assumptions generate only fear and competition that make the common good impossible. Such greed is prohibited by YHWH's kingdom of generosity.

- Israel learned from the fourth commandment that Sabbath rest is an alternative to aggressive anxiety:

> Remember the sabbath day, and keep it holy. Six days you shall labor and do all your work. But the seventh day is a sabbath to the LORD your God; you shall not do any work—you, your son or your

> daughter, your male or female slave, your live-stock, or the alien resident in your towns. For in six days the LORD made heaven and earth, the sea, and all that is in them, but rested the seventh day; therefore the LORD blessed the sabbath day and consecrated it.
>
> Exod 20:8–11

Sabbath, in the first instance, is not about worship. It is about work stoppage. It is about withdrawal from the anxiety system of Pharaoh, the refusal to let one's life be defined by production and consumption and the endless pursuit of private well-being. It is easy to imagine that in Pharaoh's system there never was a sabbath for anyone. Everyone was 24/7! The slaves never got a day off and perhaps had to multitask to meet their quotas. Pharaoh surely never took a day off; he was too busy writing memos and sending out work orders and quotas. As a result, everyone was caught up in an endless process of production and accumulation.

But at Sinai, Israel could remember one thing from the manna narrative that I have not yet mentioned. They were told not to store up bread for the next day. But there is an exception to that rule made only for Sabbath:

> "See! The LORD has given you the sabbath, therefore on the sixth day he gives you food for two days; each of you stay where you are; do not leave your place on the seventh day." So the people rested on the seventh day.
>
> Exod 16:29–30

What a surprise! Even in the wilderness where there is no extra bread at all, provision is made for Sabbath. Even in the desperate context of wilderness, work stoppage is definitional because the God of Sinai wants energy invested in the neighborhood and not in self-securing in order to get ahead, as in the empire. Of course there were cheats who multitasked on Sabbath, thereby to get a leg up on bread. But the provision of Sinai is otherwise; Sabbath is an occasion for community enhancement, for eating together and remembering and hoping and singing and dancing and telling stories—all exercises that have no production value. Israel learned at Sinai, and most especially in the fourth command on Sabbath, that there is a viable way to organize the neighborhood outside the rat race.

The Israelites departed Sinai with a new possibility. They were able to dream of enough for all, a dream that refused the common and recurring nightmares of scarcity. To be sure, there is enough yet in ancient Israel of violence and exploitation of all kinds. But now the word has been uttered; the bread has been given and broken; the commandments have been received; the Sabbath has been celebrated. Israel and its allies in covenant have stayed on the path away from Pharaoh and toward the neighborhood. Eventually the Torah was moved from Sinai to Jerusalem. In Jerusalem came new poets who extended the covenantal vision of the common good that had been ceded at Sinai. For out of Sinai, via Jerusalem, has come a rich scenario of the common good, of peaceable well-being:

> In days to come
>   the mountain of the LORD's house
> shall be established as the highest of the mountains,
>   and shall be raised up above the hills.
> Peoples shall stream to it,
>   and many nations shall come and say:

"Come, let us go up to the mountain of the LORD,
    to the house of the God of Jacob;
that he may teach us his ways
    and that we may walk in his paths."
For out of Zion shall go forth instruction,
    and the word of the LORD from Jerusalem.
He shall judge between many peoples,
    and shall arbitrate between strong nations far
        away;
they shall beat their swords into plowshares,
    and their spears into pruning hooks;
nation shall not lift up sword against nation,
    neither shall they learn war any more;
but they shall all sit under their
        own vines and under their own fig trees,
    and no one shall make them afraid;
    for the mouth of the LORD of hosts has spoken.
                                                Mic 4:1–4

It is all of a piece! There is an alternative! Recipients of overwhelming abundance can redirect their energies away from fearful anxiety to investment in the common good of the neighborhood.

V

From this narrative we draw these peculiar claims:

1. Persons living in *a system of anxiety and fear*—and consequently greed—have no time or energy for the common good. Defining anxiety focuses total attention on the self at the expense of the common good.

2. *An immense act of generosity* is required in order to break the death grip of the system of fear, anxiety, and greed.

3. Those who are immersed in such immense gifts of generosity are able to get their minds off themselves and can be *about the work of the neighborhood.* Children of such enormous abundance are able to receive new commandments that are about the well-being of the neighbor and not about the entitlements of the self.

VI

So now some conclusions. I have walked slowly through an ancient narrative memory. But my purpose is not focused on an ancient memory. It is, rather, to suggest that this ancient narrative memory is as contemporary and as urgent as our own life in the world now:

1. It is clear, is it not, that the *kingdom of paucity* and its propelling ideology of anxiety are alive and well and aggressive among us. In the United States, it takes the form of a national security state in which we are to be engaged in perpetual war—literal, ideological, and economic—in order to impose our will on others, in order to claim the resources and develop the markets to our advantage. We are not inclined or even able to speak of the national security state frontally. Most often we speak of symptoms and consequences—racial injustice, sleepless nights, lost jobs, wounded soldiers, disabled economy—but we do not name and identify the core ideology that produces our social disability. Our immediate experience of the *kingdom of scarcity* is our *entitled consumerism* in which there is always a hope for more, in which those of us on top (or striving to be) imagine that something more will make us more

comfortable, safer, and happier.[5] The ideology of consumer militarism is totally pervasive in our culture, fostered by a media that has largely polarized to serve the interests of its siloed constituents, by a judicial system that is now committed to a national security state bound up in tribalism, by aggressive TV advertising that is simply a liturgical adjunct to consumer ideology, by a star system of performance and sports figures that invites all to a fantasy that is remote from any neighborly facts on the ground. The measure of commitment to that kingdom of scarcity is the force of credit card debt that is designed to produce dependency and eventually poverty, accentuating an ever-widening wealth gap and creating a pool of cheap labor that is trapped in low-paying jobs. All of that, I submit, is inchoate in the exodus narrative in which Pharaoh is a representative figure of the nightmare of scarcity.

2. There is an alternative to the kingdom of paucity—the practice of neighborhood. It is a covenantal commitment to the common good. Such an alternative is not an easy one, because the kingdom of scarcity is totalizing in its claim. The biblical narrative, and much that is derivative from that narrative, is a sustained insistence on an alternative. That alternative is not easy or obvious or automatic. It requires a *departure*, an intentional departure from that system that the Bible terms "exodus." In that ancient narrative, the Israelites did not want to go, and once they had gone, they wished to resubmit to Pharaoh. The departure is a piece of demanding, sustained work. The capacity to think and imagine and act and live beyond that system requires imagination that has dimensions of the psychological, the economic, and the liturgical. Indeed, the core liturgy of Israel (Passover) and the

5. See Daniel McGinn, *House Lust: America's Obsession with Our Homes* (New York: Doubleday, 2008).

derivative liturgies of the church are practiced departures that now and then take on reality in the world.

While the matter is contested, I submit that theological study may well be an exercise in the art of departure, an enterprise that focuses on the great traditions of critical reflection that are resources for thinking outside the box, for making decisions to be agents in our own history and not chattel for a system of production and consumption.

3. I imagine that this narrative journey from *scarcity* through *abundance* to *neighborhood* is the key journey that Jews must make, that Christians must make, and that all humans must make in order to be maximally human. That narrative journey must be made again and again, which is why it is cast as a liturgy. It must be made again and again because the kingdom of scarcity has an immense capacity to nullify the alternative and to obliterate the journey. And therefore the journey must be taken again and again, lest we submit to the kingdom of scarcity, join the rat race, and imagine that living in a national security state is a normal environment for humanness. Such captivity of the human spirit must be again and again challenged, for it is that captivity that makes it possible

- to commit aggressive brutalizing war in the name of democratic freedom;
- to tolerate acute poverty in an economy of affluence, most especially without an adequate health-care policy;
- to defend a militarized police system that protects property over people in the name of "law and order";
- to sustain policies of abuse of the environment, all in the name of nurturing the economy;
- to transform the U.S. flag into a totem for white nationalism.

Captivation by the kingdom of scarcity requires us to live with unbearable contradictions, and, except in our better moments, those of us whose interests are protected by the system, do not take much notice of the contradiction.

4. That journey from *anxious scarcity* through *miraculous abundance* to a *neighborly common good* has been peculiarly entrusted to the church and its allies. I take "church" here to refer to the institutional church, but I mean it not as a package of truth and control but as a liturgical, interpretive offer to reimagine the world differently. When the church echoes only the world's kingdom of scarcity, then it has failed in its vocation. But the faithful church keeps at the task of living out a journey that points to the common good.

Specifically it is the Eucharist that is the great extravagant drama of the way in which the gospel of abundance overrides the claim of scarcity and invites to the common good. There is no doubt that the church's Eucharist is, among other things, simply a replay of the manna narrative in the book of Exodus. The sacrament, when not administered in coercion and anxiety, is a gesture of divine abundance that breaks the scarcity system. So consider:

- In Mark 6:30–44, Jesus came upon a crowd in a "deserted place." He has compassion on them, "for they were like sheep without a shepherd." The reference to "deserted place" and the lack of a shepherd is intentionally reminiscent of the manna narrative in the wilderness. Thus we are told,

  Jesus *took* five loaves and the two fish.
  Jesus *blessed* them.
  Jesus *broke* the loaves.
  Jesus *gave* them to the people.

The four great verbs of abundance are recited and enacted: "He took, he blessed, he broke, he gave." He fed five thousand people. He committed an overt act of abundance that broke the scarcity of the place—such an abundance that there were twelve baskets of bread left over, more than enough!

- In Mark 8:1–10, in case one missed the narrative in chapter 6, Jesus did it all over again. He came to a great crowd that was without anything to eat. He had compassion on them; the disciples wondered about "bread in the desert." Again, he enacted the four great verbs of abundance:

  Jesus *took* seven loaves.
  Jesus *gave* thanks.
  He *broke* the loaves.
  He *gave* the bread to his disciples.

Mark reports that he fed four thousand people—such an abundance!—seven baskets of bread left over—loaves abound!

- After these two feedings, Jesus, the master teacher, invites his disciples to reflect on what they have seen. They are in a boat together. They have forgotten the bread, not remembering that Jesus is in the abundance business. Jesus asks the disciples hard questions to which they make no response:

  "Why are you talking about having no bread? Do you still not perceive or understand? Are your hearts hardened? Do you have eyes, and fail to see? Do you have ears, and fail to hear? And do you not remember?"

  Mark 8:17–18

He wants them to reflect on his work of abundance. But they avoided eye contact and make no response. The disciples are beyond their interpretive capacity, because they do not know what to make of the new abundance caused by Jesus.

Like a good teacher, Jesus retreats to more concrete operational questions:

- How many baskets of bread were left over in chapter 6 when I fed five thousand?
- They are eager with an answer: "Twelve."
- How many baskets of bread were left over in chapter 8 when I fed four thousand?
- They are eager with an answer: "Seven!"

The disciples are very good at concrete, operational questions. They know the data, but they have no sense of its significance. The narrative concludes with one of Jesus' saddest verdicts:

Do you not yet understand?
Mark 8:21

Do you not understand that the ideology of *scarcity* has been broken, overwhelmed by the divine gift of *abundance*?

It is our propensity, in society and in church, to trust the narrative of scarcity. That is what makes us greedy, and exclusive, and selfish, and coercive. Even the Eucharist can be made into an occasion of scarcity, as though there were not enough for all. Such scarcity leads to exclusion at the table, even as scarcity leads to exclusion from economic life.

But the narrative of abundance persists among us. Those who sign on and depart the system of anxious scarcity become the history makers in the neighborhood. These are the ones not exhausted by Sabbath-less production who have enough energy to dream and hope. From dreams and hopes come such neighborly miracles as good health care, good schools, good housing, good care for the earth, and disarmament. The dream subverts Pharaoh's nightmare. Jesus laid it out, having read the exodus narrative:

"Do not be anxious"—do not trust Pharaoh;
"Your heavenly father knows what you need"—
then provides abundantly;
"Seek the kingdom"—care for the neighborhood,
and all will be well.

Matt 6:25-33

The ones who receive the gift have energy beyond themselves for the sake of the world. And we, if we receive well, may be among those who push beyond ourselves.

Chapter 2

THE CONTINUING SUBVERSION OF ALTERNATIVE POSSIBILITY

From Sinai to Current Covenanting

There is a contest of narratives going on in our society that is urgent, passionate, and often mean-spirited. In this contest, the world can be rendered in very different ways that yield very different assurances and very different requirements. It is a very old contest, already formed and articulated in ancient Israel, a contest in which that ancient community found no settled resolution. As ancient as it is, it is also a quite contemporary contest, one in which the shape of our society is at stake, one in which the character and the conduct of the church is at stake. And because we tend to be preoccupied with immediately pressing issues, we tend not to notice or linger over the narrative milieu in which immediate issues are situated and by which they are defined. In what follows I propose to trace this contest of narratives through the Old Testament and then to reflect on the demanding contemporaneity of that ancient exercise.

I

The ancient narrative account of reality that Israel prized and that it continued to retell for the sake of the grandchildren (Exod 10:1–2) is that YHWH, the creator of heaven and earth, had rescued slaves and overthrown oppressive

37

economics in the regime of Pharaoh. Israel made a break from Pharaoh's system of despair, a break through which YHWH was glorified and enhanced. It is clear in the Jewish practice of Passover that the exodus memory, whatever may be its historical rootage, became a paradigmatic narrative through which all social reality is described and reexperienced.[1] That is, the narrative pertains to a one-time remembered social upheaval caused by God's holiness; but the narrative looks beyond that one-time memory to see that the same transactions of oppression and emancipation continue everywhere to evoke holy power. The exodus narrative concerns the passion of *holy power* in response to *human cry*.[2] Israel is always in the context of cry, and Israel is always departing from such context. The narrative moves out beyond Israel to see that this is the narrative quality of the entire human historical process.[3]

II

In the Old Testament, it remained for the tradition of Deuteronomy to codify and institutionalize that narrative mem-

---

1. The term *paradigmatic* is used by Erich Voegelin, *Order and History,* vol. 1, *Israel and Revelation* (Baton Rouge: Louisiana State University Press, 1956), 12–22, as a contrast to *pragmatic, positivistic, critical* history. For the same quality of Israel's tradition, David Weiss Halivni uses the term *pragmatic;* on his work, see Peter Ochs, "Talmudic Scholarship as Textual Reasoning: Halivni's Pragmatic Historiography," in *Textual Reasonings: Jewish Philosophy and Text Study at the End of the Twentieth Century,* ed. Peter Ochs and Nancy Levene (Grand Rapids: Eerdmans, 2002), 120–43. For a broader consideration of these same issues, see Yosef Hayim Yerushalmi, *Zakhor: Jewish History and Jewish Memory* (Seattle: University of Washington Press, 1982).

2. See James L. Kugel, *The God of Old: Inside the Lost World of the Bible* (New York: Free Press, 2003), 109–36.

3. Jon D. Levenson, *The Hebrew Bible, the Old Testament, and Historical Criticism* (Louisville, KY: Westminster John Knox, 1993), 127–59, has warned against taking the exodus narrative beyond the claims of Israel and thereby dissolving its particularity. Levenson himself, however, acknowledges its legitimate usage in some derivative ways in other contexts.

ory of the exodus in order to make it a charter for ordering society.[4] It is the book of Deuteronomy that classically reimagines life in the world as a neighborly passing for the common good. The particular *memory* in the narrative is transposed in Deuteronomy into a set of *commandments* that provide the first move toward a social safety net in the history of the world.

The exodus-Sinai memory produces an uncommon social ethic:

- Debts owed by the poor are to be canceled after seven years so that there is no permanent underclass (Deut 15:1–18): "Remember that you were a slave in the land of Egypt, and the LORD your God redeemed you" (v. 15).
- No interest is to be charged on loans to members of the community (Deut 23:19–20).
- Permanent hospitality is to be extended to runaway slaves (Deut 23:15–16).
- No collateral is to be required on loans made to poor people (Deut 24:10–13).
- No withholding of wages that are due to the poor (Deut 24:14–15).
- No injustice toward a resident alien or an orphan (Deut 24:17–18): "Remember that you were a slave in Egypt and the LORD your God redeemed you from there" (v. 18).

---

4. On Deuteronomy as a vehicle of polity, see Norbert Lohfink, "Distribution of the Functions of Power," in *Great Themes from the Old Testament,* trans. Ronald Walls (Edinburgh: T. & T. Clark, 1982), 55–75; and S. Dean McBride, "Polity of the Covenant People: The Book of Deuteronomy," in *Constituting the Community: Studies on the Polity of Ancient Israel in Honor of S. Dean McBride Jr.,* ed. John T. Strong and Steven S. Tuell (Winona Lake, IN: Eisenbrauns, 2005), 17–33.

- And perhaps most remarkable of all, the economy is to make regular provision for the needy and the marginalized:

  When you reap your harvest in your field and forget a sheaf in the field, you shall not go back to get it; it shall be left for the alien, the orphan, and the widow, so that the LORD your God may bless you in all your undertakings. When you beat your olive trees, do not strip what is left; it shall be for the alien, the orphan, and the widow.
  When you gather the grapes of your vineyard, do not glean what is left; it shall be for the alien, the orphan, and the widow. Remember that you were a slave in the land of Egypt; therefore I am commanding you to do this.

  Deut 24:19–22

The commandment names the money crops—*grain, olives,* and *grapes*—a triad that in other places is expressed as *grain, oil, and wine,* the central produce of a market economy.[5] That triad, in the imagination of the exodus-Sinai narrative, is juxtaposed to a second triad, *alien (immigrant), orphan,* and *widow,* the ones who have no power to gain access to such valuable commodities. They have no power to gain access to such commodities because the economy is defined by the categories of Pharaoh that endlessly construct barriers between *valuable commodity* and *needy consumer.* But that wall of separation is removed by this primal

---

5. It is most likely that grain, wine, and oil were the normal commercial produce of agriculture for the peasants; through a system of economic power that flowed to the urban center, however, the peasants themselves did not benefit from the production of the money crops.

exodus narrative and by the covenantal commandments that are extrapolated from it. The tradition of Deuteronomy intends to resituate the economy of Israel into the fabric of the neighborhood. In this tradition, it is not true that the economy is a freestanding autonomous system; it is, rather, checked and measured at every turn by the reality of the neighborhood.

That vision of a neighborhood is a given in ancient Israel that continued to refer back to the exodus-Sinai narrative. But it is also recognized, in the tradition itself, that in deep ways the children of the narrative resist this vision. So Moses chides his resistant listeners:

> Do not be hardhearted or tightfisted toward your needy neighbor. You should rather open your hand, willingly lending enough to meet the need, whatever it may be. Be careful that you do not entertain a mean thought, thinking, "The seventh year, the year of remission, is near," and therefore view your needy neighbor with hostility and give nothing; your neighbor might cry to the LORD against you, and you would incur guilt. Give liberally and be ungrudging when you do so, for on this account the LORD your God will bless you in all your work and in all that you undertake. Since there will never cease to be some in need on the earth, I therefore command you, "Open your hand to the poor and needy neighbor in your land."
>
> Deut 15:7–11

The propensity to hardheartedness is countered in the tradition by the memory that this economy-with-neighborhood is not just a good liberal idea. It is, rather, the intention of the God of the exodus:

Remember that you were a slave in the land of Egypt, and the LORD your God redeemed you; for this reason I lay this command upon you today.

Deut 15:15

Remember that you were a slave in Egypt, and diligently observe these statutes.

Deut 16:12

Remember that you were a slave in Egypt and the LORD your God redeemed you from there; therefore I command you to do this.

Deut 24:18

Remember that you were a slave in the land of Egypt; therefore I am commanding you to do this.

Deut 24:22

The tradition, by way of the exodus, makes a connection between YHWH, the Lord of the exodus, and the neighbor. *Love of God* comes as *love of neighbor* with an immediate, concrete, economic dimension.[6]

It is no wonder that the key question of this tradition of commandment, rooted in a memory of emancipation, is the question of the neighbor: Who is my neighbor? It is a question about which Israel quarreled and about which we continue to quarrel. Indeed, the neighbor question lingers in the narrative so powerfully that Michael Walzer, noted

6. The transposition of love of God into love of neighbor is, of course, articulated in 1 John 4:20–21. That transposition is anticipated, however, in Jer 22:15–16, wherein "knowing YHWH" is equated with justice for the poor and needy. Same difference!

Jewish political philosopher, can conclude that the exodus narrative is the taproot of all revolutions in the modern world. The Lord of Sinai intends that all economies should be renovated for the common good:

> So pharaonic oppression, deliverance, Sinai, and Canaan are still with us, powerful memories shaping our perceptions of the political world. The "door of hope" is still open; things are not what they might be—even when what they might be isn't totally different from what they are. This is a central theme in Western thought, always present though elaborated in many different ways. We still believe, or many of us do, what the Exodus first taught, or what it has commonly been taken to teach, about the meaning and possibility of politics and about its proper form:
>
> — first, that wherever you live, it is probably Egypt;
> — second, that there is a better place, a world more attractive, a promised land;
> — and third, that "the way to the land is through the wilderness." There is no way to get from here to there except by joining together and marching.[7]

So chant the children of justice:

> "We are marching, we are marching, we are marching."

---

7. Michael Walzer, *Exodus and Revolution* (New York: Basic Books, 1985), 149.

III

There is, however, a powerful *counternarrative* in the biblical tradition that resists the claims of exodus-Sinai-Deuteronomy. It is a counternarrative that resists the neighbor question, because the draw back into the fearful, anxious world of Pharaoh is enormously compelling for almost all of us. Our memory fades, and we imagine the security that Pharaoh's system offered and yearn for an imagined well-being back there.

1. The travel out of Egypt into the alternative narrative immediately produces an attack of nostalgia for the imagined good old days of Pharaoh. Israel had found the new narrative too demanding and too precarious and had failed in their feeble remembering.

2. Once they had arrived at Sinai, we can see a much more sustained effort to resist the emancipatory narrative of neighborliness; as the tradition is shaped from Mount Sinai, the purity trajectory began to tone things down. It may be that the purity traditions come late, but for our purposes, they are lodged right in the midst of the Sinai corpus itself (Exod 25–31; 35–40; Lev; Num 10:11–36:13). In the development of *holiness* as a qualification for access to God's gifts for life, there came the notion of "graded holiness," that is, there are degrees of eligibility, so some are more eligible for access than others.[8] Israel appropriates from its cultural environment a pattern of organizing holy space with three "chambers of qualification" so that there will be an outer court, a holy place, and a most holy place (holy of holies), where there is an intensity of divine

8. See Philip P. Jenson, "Graded Holiness: A Key to the Priestly Conception of the World," Journal for the Study of the Old Testament: Supplement Series 106 (Sheffield: JSOT Press, 1992).

presence and divine power. The chambers are ordered so that some are admitted only at the edge, fewer are permitted to enter midway, and only one is given access clear to the center. The process is to differentiate between neighbors, some better than others.

As close as we can come to such a notion of three chambers of qualification is a commercial airline with tourist class and first class, and the "holy of holies" where none may go (more recently protected by a very strong door).[9] But, of course, every social organization has differentiations among neighbors, sometimes regional, sometimes educational, sometimes race, class, and gender, and sometimes ideological. At Sinai, some imagined the regimentation of holiness concerned:

- *Cultic access*—which is like health-care policy—since the priests were the doctors of that time, administrators of health care.

- *Moral ratings*, good people and bad people, clean people and unclean people, a Manichean perspective that continues to vex communities, liberal and conservative, the rational and the passionate.

- *Economic possibility* for those who have access to resources and opportunity in the neighborhood. The gradations of holiness concerning economic possibility tend to turn on connectedness, being at the right place at the right time, and productivity. Consequently those who are not productive are increasingly banished from access to the goodies.

9. I have suggested this parallel between temple and plane in "The Tearing of the Curtain (Matt. 27:51)," in *Faithful Witness: A Festschrift Honoring Ronald Goetz*, ed. Michael J. Bell, H. Scott Matheney, and Dan Peerman (Elmhurst, IL: Elmhurst College, 2002), 77–83.

The resistance to the common good has *cultic, moral,* and *economic* dimensions. As a consequence, we can, in broad outline, see a collision course between the *neighborly possibilities* mandated by the tradition of Deuteronomy and the *regimentations of holiness* in the Priestly traditions. Both are in the Bible; both are at Sinai. We may imagine, moreover, that this ancient folk, like us, are of a double mind about it. They knew better, but when it came down to cases, they could not help making distinctions. Thus we may imagine that even given the exodus-Sinai narrative of an alternative to Pharaoh's system, there was a struggle concerning the neighborly good. That struggle eventuated in an interpretive contest, a contest kept alive among Jews in the rabbinic traditions of Hillel and Gamaliel, and on into our own time among contemporary orthodox and rationalistic interpretations. Contestation for the common good is an endless project. That contest is a summons and a vexation in the church, because of our own double-mindedness.

IV

The exodus-Sinai narrative for neighborliness holds center stage in the Old Testament. It is with King Solomon, however, that this narrative faces its most serious challenge. In Solomon, there is (a) a fresh *enthrallment with Egypt* and (b) a passion for *graded holiness*. There is, moreover, a deep connection between the enthrallment with Egypt and the passion for graded holiness, for Pharaoh's Egyptian society did indeed practice graded holiness with its cultic moral and economic dimensions. (See Gen 43:32 on discriminating lunch-counter practices.) Had Israel remembered better, they would have remembered more clearly what it was like back in Egypt to be graded at the lowest level and therefore denied access to economic benefit. There is something ironic about this most prominent king in ancient Israel; his name "Solomon" means shalom, but his sponsorship of a skewed royal shalom contradicts the common good:[10]

—The echoes of Pharaoh's exploitative system are everywhere evident in what we know about Solomon. For starters, the king is married to Pharaoh's daughter and surely wants to borrow from and emulate his father-in-law (see 1 Kgs 3:1; 7:8; 9:16, 24). It is most plausible that there were important imports from Egypt by Solomon, not least his policy of forced labor that inscripted people to support the aggrandizing projects of the government. That conscription we now call "the draft," but in ancient days and in ancient texts it is termed "forced labor" (1 Sam 8:10–17; 1 Kgs 5:13–18; 9:20–22). It is evident that Pharaoh's notion of the common good—a hierarchical ordering shaped like an Egyptian pyramid—reappeared in Jerusalem.

—The echoes of Pharaoh are matched by a graded holiness and by its consequent of a hierarchical ordering of society. Solomon, of course, is the great temple builder in ancient Israel. We have, in the text, what amounts to a blueprint for his temple that was an imitation of a generic type of building from his culture:

- The "outer court," in NRSV, is called "the vestibule":

     The vestibule in front of the nave of the house was twenty cubits wide, across the width of the house. Its depth was ten cubits in front of the house.

     1 Kgs 6:3

---

10. For what follows on Solomon, see Walter Brueggemann, *Solomon: Israel's Ironic Icon of Human Achievement* (Columbia: University of South Carolina Press, 2005).

- The "holy court," in NRSV, is called "the nave":

> He also built a structure against the wall of the house, running around the walls of the house, both the nave and the inner sanctuary; and he made side chambers all around. The lowest story was five cubits wide, the middle one was six cubits wide, and the third was seven cubits wide; for around the outside of the house he made offsets on the wall in order that the supporting beams should not be inserted into the walls of the house. . . . The house, that is, the nave in front of the inner sanctuary, was forty cubits long. The cedar within the house had carvings of gourds and open flowers; all was cedar, no stone was seen.
>
> 1 Kgs 6:5–6, 17–18

- The "holy of holies," in NRSV, is called "the most holy place":

> He built twenty cubits of the rear of the house with boards of cedar from the floor to the rafters, and he built this within as an inner sanctuary, as the most holy place. . . . The inner sanctuary he prepared in the innermost part of the house, to set there the ark of the covenant of the LORD. The interior of the inner sanctuary was twenty cubits long, twenty cubits wide, and twenty cubits high; he overlaid it with pure *gold*. He also overlaid the altar with cedar. Solomon overlaid the inside of the house with pure *gold*, then he drew chains of *gold* across, in front of the inner sanctuary, and overlaid it with *gold*. Next

> he overlaid the whole house with *gold*, in order
> that the whole house might be perfect; even the
> whole altar that belonged to the inner sanctuary
> he overlaid with *gold*.
>
> 1 Kgs 6:16, 19–22

I take so long with this matter because the shape of the temple wrought by Solomon is not an accidental architectural detail. It is, rather, a replica of *an imagined social order.* That the description of the temple ends with the term *gold* used six times indicates a fascination with precious commodity; by extrapolation we may conclude that Solomon's temple was committed to the commoditization of all social relationships so that we are able to see *what* is valued and, consequently, *who* is valued. (It is the shape and arrangement of airplanes, school systems, health-care delivery, housing patterns, and all the rest.)

Solomon's fascination with all things Egyptian and Solomon's zeal for the temple with its older residence for God invite us to look closely at the royal report from which we can determine a great deal about the socioeconomic claims of this narrative that stand in deep tension with the neighborly narrative of Sinai.

I will identify three aspects of this narrative of royal regime that are important for the long-term claims of faith:

1. It is clear that Solomon is committed to an accumulation of *wealth*, that everything in his hand turned commodity. The temple reeks with gold, and after his summit meeting with the Queen of Sheba, we are told:

> Thus King Solomon excelled all the kings of the
> earth in riches and in wisdom. . . . Every one of
> them brought a present, objects of silver and gold,

garments, weaponry, spices, horses, and mules, so much year by year.

1 Kgs 10:23, 25; see vv. 14-20

It may well be that the acquisitiveness and commoditization are also reflected in the report that Solomon had seven hundred princesses and three hundred concubines (1 Kgs 11:3). The numbers might suggest that this throng of women were used, if not for sexual purposes, then surely for political purposes through a network of alliances.

2. It is clear that Solomon is committed to *power*. It is evident that his power was linked to his wealth. His enormous power is expressed in the fact that he was an arms dealer, a middleman passing horses and chariots between north and south:

Solomon's import of horses was from Egypt and Kue, and the king's traders received them from Kue at a price. A chariot could be imported from Egypt for six hundred shekels of silver, and a horse for one hundred fifty; so through the king's traders they were exported to all the kings of the Hittites and the kings of Aram.

1 Kgs 10:28-29

It is astonishing that much arms traffic, then and now, is not in the service of any policy; it is, rather, simply a way of financial leverage. Alongside Solomon's traffic in armaments, he had immense commercial interest (1 Kgs 9:26-28), plus a system of collecting protection money from a variety of sources:

Solomon was sovereign over all the kingdoms from the Euphrates to the land of the Philistines, even to the border of Egypt; they brought tribute and served Solomon all the days of his life.

1 Kgs 4:21

His commercial power was matched and reinforced by his military power, as he kept a standing army of chariots and cavalry and built immense fortresses at the key locations of Hazor, Gezer, and Megiddo:

> This is the account of the forced labor that King Solomon conscripted to build the house of the LORD and his own house, the Millo and the wall of Jerusalem, Hazor, Megiddo, Gezer... so Solomon rebuilt Gezer, Lower Beth-horon, Baalath, Tamar in the wilderness, within the land, as well as all of Solomon's storage cities, the cities for his chariots, the cities for his cavalry, and whatever Solomon desired to build, in Jerusalem, in Lebanon, and in all the land of his dominion.
>
> 1 Kgs 9:15, 17–19

The practice of forced labor, commoditization, traffic in arms, and commerce through trade agreements all converged to make Solomon a major political force in his world, a fact attested by his meeting with the Queen of Sheba that was surely a summit concerning trade agreements (1 Kgs 10:1–10). Solomon did indeed fashion a national security state!

3. Solomon is a great practitioner of *wisdom*. It is reported that he composed three hundred proverbs and one hundred and five songs:

> He would speak of trees, from the cedar that is in the Lebanon to the hyssop that grows in the wall; he would speak of animals, and birds, and reptiles, and

fish. People came from all the nations to hear the wisdom of Solomon; they came from all the kings of the earth who had heard of his wisdom.

1 Kgs 4:33–34

We may take this as his personal achievement. More likely it is a celebration of Solomon as a patron of the arts, not unlike having Isaac Stern at the White House. Solomon's artists included the poets of wisdom who were able to codify what became scientific data concerning "creation." The quest for "wisdom" may have been (a) in order to appear as champion of the arts that would enhance the regime, (b) the development of the arts and skills of governance that depended on a practice of discernment, and (c) the accumulation of data so that the elite had a monopoly on "intelligence." All of these interests in art, governance, and intelligence converge in "wisdom" for which Solomon is noted. While such wisdom may have a theological component, given Solomon's pursuit of wealth and power, we may take "wisdom" here in a more cynical sense as a practice of control. Solomon is celebrated for his worldly awareness, perhaps in the same way as the "wise men" that clustered around Lyndon Johnson and Richard Nixon, of whom Henry Kissinger is the last prominent survivor.[11] These are the ones, then and now, who knew everything but in the end failed to understand anything:

The whole earth sought the presence of Solomon to hear his wisdom, which God had put into his mind.

1 Kgs 10:24

11. On such failed "wisdom," see Walter Isaacson and Evan Thomas, *The Wise Men: Six Friends and the World They Made* (New York: Simon & Schuster, 1988).

Solomon understood how the world worked, probed the mysteries, and kept on his payroll the academics who could advance his control, his prestige, and his security.

There is a reason that Solomon is so celebrated and so widely admired. He is, as remembered in the narrative, the prominent man, "the man," who embodies *the best* control of the world, for what is better than a collage of *wealth*, *power*, and *wisdom*! The consequence is that one can have the world on one's own terms.

Now having summarized all of that as a counternarrative that by design and in effect resisted the exodus-Sinai narrative, I conclude my comment on Solomon with an interesting footnote. At the beginning of the Solomon narrative, there is an ironic report on the handover of power from the father David to his son Solomon. In 1 Kings 2:2–4, David soberly admonishes Solomon to keep the Torah as the basis of the throne. This advice from David is followed immediately with David's urging to Solomon that he immediately and systematically execute his enemies in the government, Joab and Shimei (2:5–8). It is reported, moreover, that Solomon palpably did so, eliminating not only Joab and Shimei, as David had urged (2:28–46), but also his brother Adonijah (2:13–25), a rival for the family throne.

What interests us is that in the midst of these assassinations enacted in order to secure the throne, there is a brief paragraph about Abiathar, the priest who had opposed Solomon's kingship (see 1 Kgs 1:7). He is a dangerous opponent of Solomon, but you cannot kill a priest . . . yet! Instead of a death sentence, Abiathar is banished by Solomon away from the capital city to his home village, where he cannot do any harm to the regime:

The king said to the priest Abiathar, "Go to Anathoth, to your estate; for you deserve death. But I will not at this time put you to death, because you carried the ark of the Lord GOD before my father David, and because you shared in all the hardships my father endured." So Solomon banished Abiathar from being priest to the LORD, thus fulfilling the word of the LORD that he had spoken concerning the house of Eli in Shiloh.

1 Kgs 2:26–27

Abiathar departs the regime of *wealth, power, and wisdom* and is marginalized in his innocent, remote village, there to watch the regime and to brood about its commitments to distortion. He will have a very long time to brood . . . but I will leave that for now.

V

Solomon is the model in the Bible for a global perspective of the common good, a perspective that smacks of *privilege*, *entitlement*, and *exploitation*, all in the name of the God of the three-chambered temple, the three chambers that partition social life and social resources into *the qualified, the partially qualified*, and *the disqualified*. It takes little critical imagination to see that Solomon's perspective, which came to dominate urban Israel's imagination, is an act of resistance against the neighborly demands of Sinai and an alternative to the possibilities of Mount Sinai. It is as though Pharaoh, through his son-in-law, had come to rule in Israel as in Egypt. Jerusalem becomes a place that reenacts Pharaoh's acquisitiveness that is rooted in Pharaoh's anxieties.

That perspective of Pharaoh-via-Solomon takes on a powerful life in Jerusalem, largely nullifying the vision of Sinai. In the end, it is as though the exodus had never happened. Or as Moses says, at the end of the book of Deuteronomy in the ultimate covenant curse, it is as though the alternative possibility for God's people is to end, yet again, in Egypt:

> The LORD will bring you back in ships to Egypt, by a route that I promised you would never see again; and there you shall offer yourselves for sale to your enemies as male and female slaves, but there will be no buyer.
>
> Deut 28:68

Pharaoh always prevails! Except that Sinai continues to have its advocates. The advocates in ancient Israel are not shrill administrators. They are, rather, poets who imagine outside the box, who, by their very lives, attest that the world can be organized differently. You know the roll call of those poets who did not give in to Pharaoh. The list is short!

- *Nathan,* who by way of parable faced Solomonic, pharaonic King David (2 Sam 12:1–5);
- *Elijah,* reckoned as "troubler" and "enemy" in Israel (1 Kgs 18:17; 21:20), who dealt with Solomonic, pharaonic Ahab;
- *Amos,* who grieved a failed society in his confrontation with Solomonic, pharaonic Amaziah (Amos 7:10–17).

The prophets were not great liberals. They were, rather, *poets* outside the box who were rooted in Sinai, who were gifted with uncommon imagination, and who operated on the astonishing notion that the claims of the exodus God who had created heaven and earth were not easily overcome or dismissed. They were, each in a distinct style and context, convinced that the common good was ill served by Solomon's chambers of qualification or by pharaonic notions of cheap labor in the interest of a predatory economy.

VI

If one studies the Old Testament, one can see a collision course in ancient Israel, long in coming but certainly not to be escaped. The Jerusalem enterprise was increasingly narcoticized by its sense of entitlement; it imagined itself exempt from the starchy requirements of the historical process, and so delivered to its beneficiaries a wondrous entitlement of privilege and security under the aegis of a patron God.

But the poets notice! And if you draw the Old Testament down toward the totalizing crisis of the destruction of Jerusalem in 587 BCE, akin to a nationwide threat of pandemic, you eventually will come to the prophet Jeremiah, who, in his poetic daring, had to preside over his own national devastation—for it takes a poet to comprehend such profound loss! Imagine, it is not the managers, not the ideologues, not the social activists, not the shrill moralists, right or left, but the poets who are able (and compelled!) to go to the depth of the crisis and to reach deep into God's own conflicted heart.[12]

---

12. On the decisive role of the poet in the construction of society, see Walter Brueggemann, *Finally Comes the Poet: Daring Speech for Proclamation* (Minneapolis: Fortress Press, 1989).

Jeremiah is a village guy with not very impressive credentials. The book of Jeremiah begins with his pedigree:

> The words of Jeremiah son of Hilkiah, of the priests who were in Anathoth in the land of Benjamin.
>
> Jer 1:1

He is the son of Hilkiah, a priest. He was from the land of Benjamin, just across the northern border from Judah and Jerusalem, close enough to see, far enough to be unencumbered. Hilkiah, his father, we may know only from one other text. Perhaps he was the priest who helped recover the scroll of Deuteronomy for King Josiah (2 Kgs 22:8–13). Benjamin we know in ancient geography. But in that opening line, between Hilkiah and Benjamin stands . . . Anathoth! The utterance of the word *Anathoth* sets off among us an exegetical alarm. We know of this village hometown; we reel through our exegetical memory bank and push back to the verses concerning Solomon's seizure of power. The verdict of the aggressive new king to the honored old priest Abiathar:

> Go to Anathoth, to your estate; for you deserve death.
>
> 1 Kgs 2:26

Abiathar went to Anathoth, defrocked from Jerusalem, still a rural priest acting as a village pastor. He had sons, and sons of sons. They were, like him, priests. They did that for four hundred years. Every day, for four hundred years, they looked to the southern horizon of the village. They could see traces of Jerusalem, and they heard the reports. They heard reports of forced labor and armaments and political marriages and exploitation and foolishness of a hundred kinds. Coming from the city were the mantras that mingled exclusive religion and patriotic exceptionalism, affirmations about *unconditional promise* (2 Sam 7:15–16), and an *uninterrupted divine presence* (1 Kgs 8:12–13) (and "bombs bursting in air and rockets' red glare"), and abusive labor policy and despair and anxiety and self-sufficiency and amnesia and, finally, an illusion. It took four hundred years to gather together a sinking sense of an ending.

At the end of four hundred years, this son of exiled Abiathar—many generations later—this son of exiles from Jerusalem, this Jeremiah, showed up in Jerusalem yet again. He showed up there with words:

> The words of Jeremiah son of Hilkiah, of the priests who were in Anathoth in the land of Benjamin.
>
> Jer 1:1

The man from Anathoth has his own words: "Jeremiah, . . . to whom the word of the LORD came" (1:1–2). He has spent four hundred years transposing *the word of the LORD* into *the words of Jeremiah*. It was a word evoked exactly for this moment. He addresses the kings who managed the establishment:

> . . . in the days of King Josiah son of Amon of Judah, in the thirteenth year of his reign. It came also in the days of King Jehoiakim son of Josiah of Judah.
>
> Jer 1:2–3

It was a word to the establishment that could see beyond the kings so that his opener ended this way:

> . . . until the end of the eleventh year of King Zedekiah son of Josiah of Judah, until the captivity of Jerusalem in the fifth month.
>
> Jer 1:3

This is a word from the banished poet to the kings, until their royal displacement. The poet brings only words. But what else will matter when the city crackles in flames and the leadership is seized by an ending that they did not see coming? Jeremiah and his family had watched—for four hundred years—and had long since seen a trajectory of death. That trajectory was marked by

- Solomonic wealth: "gold, gold, gold";
- Solomonic power, so that there was no one like him, before or since (1 Kgs 3:12);
- Solomonic wisdom, ample proverbs, and files of intelligence.

It was a trajectory to death. It was a long-term practice of the lethal. Opposition and resistance to the lethal does not require more technology or more advocacy or more activism. It simply evokes words of a special sort:

> The words of Jeremiah . . . to whom the word of the Lord came.

VII

Jeremiah, with a deep breath, decisively counters the primal commitments of the Jerusalem establishment. We can see in one poetic-prophetic utterance the collision of these two perceptions of reality. Here is the poem:

> Thus says the LORD: Do not let the wise boast in their *wisdom*, do not let the mighty boast in their *might*, do not let the wealthy boast in their *wealth*; but let those who boast boast in this; that they understand and know me, that I am the LORD; I act with *steadfast love*, *justice*, and *righteousness* in the earth, for in these things I delight, says the LORD.
>
> Jer 9:23–24

The poem is in five parts. I spend time on it, because I have come to think that these are the verses that provide the clue to the ancient crisis in Jeremiah's time and perhaps to our own time and place as God's people:

1. Jeremiah lines out *the lethal commitments* that are at work in the Jerusalem establishment:

> Do not praise wealth.
> Do not praise might.
> Do not praise wisdom.

The term *boast*—"do not let the wise boast"—is the Hebrew term *hallel*, as in *hallelu-jah*, "praise YHWH." Do not commend or celebrate these qualities of life.

It is as though, in this triad of wealth, might, and wisdom, the poet has simply taken a page from Solomon's playbook. You will remember Solomon's inventory of achievements:

- enough *wisdom* to control the mystery and to reduce it to a technical operation;

- enough *might* to build a national security state in the middle of the Fertile Crescent;
- enough *wealth* to satisfy every acquisitive appetite.

Enough of wisdom, might, and wealth; and says Jeremiah, "Don't brag on it!"

2. There is, says the village poet, *an alternative*:

> . . . but let those who boast boast in this; that they understand and know me, that I am the LORD.
>
> Jer 9:24

Now the term *hallel* might be "praise" rather than "boast." The big issue in the "boast" that is now recommended is that it refers to YHWH, the God of the exodus. The double list of "boasts" is an *either/or* in ancient Jerusalem, mutually exclusive, YHWH or the Solomonic triad. But this alternative is more than a claim for YHWH; it is also a claim for Israel. Israel is the community that "knows YHWH," that is privy to YHWH's purpose in the world and has committed to YHWH. As a result, Israel "understands" YHWH, reflects deeply on who YHWH is. The "or" of the "either/or" is to meditate on the Torah, which constitutes the ground of knowledge and discernment concerning YHWH. Imagine that—something Pharaoh never thought about and over which Solomon never lingered, access to YHWH's own life in the world.

3. The end of the sentence is "*I am YHWH.*" In the world of wealth, might, and wisdom, everyone is an object or a commodity that occurs at the end of the sentence. But when YHWH occurs at the end of a sentence in that frame of reference, YHWH is transposed into a lifeless idol. That is what Solomon sought and finally accomplished in his third

chamber—a God settled, under control, tamed to a favorite ideology, echo of a preferred social passion. But not here in Jeremiah. Here *YHWH is the subject and not the object*, an agent and not a commodity, a force of will and not an idol. Thus the text has YHWH say, "I am YHWH who. . . ." I am YHWH who creates heaven and earth; I am YHWH who brought you out of the land of Egypt. I am YHWH who heals all your diseases and forgives all your sins. I am YHWH who creates and re-creates. Such a God cannot function easily in a world of three-chambered qualification, of systemic and absolute control. Such a God lives in tension with the royal triad and with pet projects of any sort.

4. YHWH is the one *with active verbs*. YHWH is the one with remarkable adjectives:

> I act with steadfast love, justice, and righteousness in the earth, for in these things I delight, says the LORD.
> Jer 9:24

So here is YHWH's triad, which we first might state in Hebrew: *ḥesed, mišpaṭ, ṣedaqah.*

- *Steadfast love (ḥesed)* is to stand in solidarity, to honor commitments, to be reliable toward all the partners.
- *Justice (mišpaṭ)* in the Old Testament concerns distribution in order to make sure that all members of the community have access to resources and goods for the sake of a viable life of dignity. In covenantal tradition, the particular subject of YHWH's justice is the triad "widow, orphan, immigrant," those without leverage or muscle to sustain their own legitimate place in society.

- *Righteousness* (*ṣedaqah*) concerns active intervention in social affairs, taking an initiative to intervene effectively in order to rehabilitate society, to respond to social grievance, and to correct every humanity-diminishing activity.

This triad, *ḥesed*, *mišpaṭ*, and *ṣedaqah*, is everywhere present in Old Testament talk about divine purpose and about Israel's covenantal life in the world. The terms, moreover, overlap and cover for one another so that when any one of them occurs in the text, we may extrapolate to the others. The God of Israel, unlike the gods of Egypt, is committed to the covenantal project of each in solidarity for all. And Israel, pledged to YHWH, is committed to the same project.

5. Finally, Jeremiah has God say at the end of the passage,

> In these things—in *ḥesed*, in *mišpaṭ*, in *ṣedaqah*—
> *I delight.*

The term *delight* is a word used in prophetic poetry to describe the kinds of offerings and sacrifices that are offered in worship that will please YHWH. Indeed, it is the same term used in Hosea 6:6, where the prophet prioritizes covenantal solidarity over cultic activity:

> For I *desire* steadfast love and not sacrifice,
>   the knowledge of God rather than burnt offerings.

This text, moreover, is reiterated twice by Jesus:

- In Matthew 9:13, in the debate over eating with tax collectors and sinners:

> Go and learn what this means, "I *desire* mercy, not sacrifice." For I have come to call not the righteous but sinners.

- In Matthew 12:7, with the debate over healing on the Sabbath:

> But if you had known what this means, "I *desire* mercy and not sacrifice," you would not have condemned the guiltless.

In Jeremiah 9, in Hosea 6, and twice in the teaching of Jesus according to Matthew, it is the faithful well-being of the human community that is *well pleasing to YHWH:*

- YHWH loves steadfast covenantal solidarity.
- YHWH loves justice that gives access and viability to the weak.
- YHWH loves righteousness as intervention for social well-being.

And, says the prophet, you in covenant are the ones who can brag on this, that you have been given the secret of God's primal impulse.

VIII

Now the two triads offered by Jeremiah constitute *the decisive either/or* of faith in ancient Israel and of faith in the derivative story of humanity:

- *either:* wisdom, might, and wealth;
- *or:* steadfast love, justice, righteousness.

One is a triad of *death* because it violates neighborliness. The other is a triad of *life* because it coheres with YHWH's best intention for all creation. In prophetic discourse, there is no compromise on this either/or, no middle ground. It is a contestation that is designed to place all serious persons, liberal and conservative, in profound crisis. It is the purpose of the poetry to invite the listener into serious contestation where we may, always again, redecide about our common life in the world.

In that ancient moment of Jeremiah, it is clear that his poetry is vindicated by the course of events. This village voice from Anathoth was able to trace, right from Solomon down to the end, the way in which the Jerusalem commitment to an economy based on fear, anxiety, scarcity, acquisitiveness, and control had fated Israel to sociopolitical failure. Of course, it is a daring poetic inference that such a failure about the economy produced the end of Jerusalem at the hands of Babylon. But so the argument goes in a world where YHWH is said to be Lord of the public process. In the grief of YHWH and in the pathos of Jeremiah, it is clear that the royal, priestly apparatus never gave the time of day to economic possibilities based in social solidarity. As the poet lived through Israel's experience of destruction, termination, and displacement, not unlike the trauma and failure of national nerve in response to the pandemics of coronavirus, racial injustice, and wealth inequality, Jeremiah knew that the collision course rooted in Solomon had now come to fruition. He was left to do *the poetry, the grief, the dread,* and, eventually, *the hope.*

IX

It remains to move from this narrative account of social collision to our own time and place. I will do so with four extrapolations:

1. This summary of matters in these two verses from Jeremiah exhibit *Sinai* and *Solomon* as major alternatives. In a move to the memory of the church, we may read this either/or toward the New Testament. In his opening assertions in 1 Corinthians 1, Paul ends his argument in 1:31 this way:

> in order that, as it is written, "Let the one who boasts, boast in the Lord."
>
> 1 Cor 1:31

These words are an exact quote from our verses in Jeremiah, a quotation that indicates that Paul understands his own argument and the condition of the church in Corinth as parallel to that of ancient Israel in Jeremiah's time. In his first chapter of 1 Corinthians, we can see how the same contestation works. It is a statement of Paul's theology of the cross in which he concludes:

> For God's foolishness is wiser than human wisdom,
> and God's weakness is stronger than human strength.
>
> 1 Cor 1:25

Paul celebrates God's foolishness in the cross that is wiser than human *wisdom*; he celebrates God's weakness on the cross that is stronger than human *might*. In his argument, Paul picks up two of Jeremiah's three terms, *wisdom* and *might*. Jeremiah's third term, *wealth*, is not given here. But wealth is the topic of Paul's sermon to the church in 2 Corinthians 8. Paul discusses the church offering and the issue of poverty and wealth. In that discourse, he issues a stunning assertion of Jesus' poverty against human wealth:

> For you know the generous act of our Lord Jesus Christ, that though he was rich, yet for your sakes he became poor, so that by his poverty you might become rich.
>
> 2 Cor 8:9

If we take the poverty/wealth assertion of this chapter and align it with the other two in 1 Corinthians 1, we get the same triad for Jesus, *foolishness*, *weakness*, and *poverty*, that are offered as contradictions to the world's overvaluing of *wisdom*, *might*, and *wealth*. Thus Paul instructs the church on the proper matters about which to boast, and then he writes:

> Consider your own call.
>
> 1 Cor 1:26

It is not a call to worldly wisdom, worldly wealth, or worldly power. For it is the alternative remembered in Israel and exhibited in Jesus' life, death, and resurrection that constitutes a summons to the church and a clue to the future of the world. Paul is able to reiterate the poetry of Jeremiah as it is enacted in the body of Jesus. He bids that it be reenacted in the body of Christ.

2. The radical either/or,

- of Sinai and Solomon,
- of Jeremiah 9:23–24,
- of Paul in 1 and 2 Corinthians,

positions the church vis-à-vis the political economy of the United States. It is clear that we have been on our way, since Teddy Roosevelt, to the formation of a national security state that has long postured as an empire. It is clear that the U.S. national security state thrives on wisdom, might, and wealth. That triad of commitments, moreover, gets articulated among us both as aggressive militarized police action and as unrestrained self-indulgent consumer entitlement in which liberals and conservatives together have taken for granted our privileged status in the world as God's most recently chosen people.

In that context that is defining for all of us who are liberals and conservatives, there is implicit a clear summons to the covenanted people of God to be in acute tension with the theological trajectory of a national security state recently supercharged by tribalism and the rhetoric of America First. We are commonly and vaguely against "the war," of course, and more obvious violations perpetrated by the state, such as separating children from their parents at the border. We do a lesser job on the sense of consumer entitlement that those of us who are economically advantaged and our children inhale daily and that we take thoughtlessly as our birthright. If this analysis and this extrapolation are in any way correct, then the present and coming troubles of our society call us away from our internal struggles in the church in order that the church may address these great public missional issues. It remains to be seen how the church can fashion an intentional alternative to the national security state, which is itself a path to death. The critical edge of faith requires us to ask if a national security state can be impinged on and transformed by strands of neighborly commitment that lie deep in our national history.[13]

3. I am obligated before I finish to ask how this summons to alternative might impact our way of thinking critically about ministry. I had these four thoughts:

—The "or" of *hesed*, *mišpaṭ*, and *ṣedaqah* is an invitation to *allow for God's holiness* as an active, transformative,

---

13. On that neighborly commitment in our national history, see the classic statement of Robert N. Bellah, *The Broken Covenant: American Civil Religion in Time of Trial* (New York: Seabury, 1975).

dynamic agency in the world. This text, now as then, is a summons to contest and is to be seriously engaged. The impulse toward covenantal fidelity is an enormously active one that cannot be slotted as "business as usual." The claim behind the summons is that being out of sync with this holy Agency is lethal.

—Our capacity to understand, explain, and thereby control is broken by the concrete bodily reality of embraced pain. None of our theological reasoning has a reliable resolution to the questions of theodicy and the force of unmerited pain. Such pain is dealt with only by embrace as body touches body in compassion. The testimony of this textual tradition is that God's holiness embraces pain and that God's holiness forms an alliance with pain that cuts underneath every explanation we may offer. There is a theological tradition of apatheia in which God does not suffer. But the entire biblical tradition dissents from such cleanness; from the earliest response of YHWH to the cry of the Egyptian slaves, it is clear that the Holy One can say:

> I have observed the misery of my people who are in Egypt; I have heard their cry on account of their taskmasters. Indeed, I know their sufferings, and I have come down to deliver them from the Egyptians.
> Exod 3:7–8

Such an alliance requires us to reimagine pain in completely new ways as the central marking of the world; it requires us, moreover, to reimagine the Holy One as the one decisively impinged on by the pain of the world.

—The alliance of holiness with pain generates reliable truthfulness. This disturbing claim flies in the face of much of our intellectual history in the West that imagines that truth is set out beyond the embarrassment of pain as a foolproof system of control. But in the rendezvous of God's holiness with worldly pain, this truthfulness becomes a dissent from our controlling knowledge. Indeed, in his familiar lyric, Paul is highly suspicious of the claims of knowledge:

> If I ... understand all mysteries and all knowledge ... but do not have love. ...
>
> 1 Cor 13:2

This truth will be insistent upon us,

> as long as too many people compete for too few resources;
> as long as we ingest and defecate and get bowel blockages;
> as long as we copulate and have failed erections;
> as long as we die and kill and suffer and wait.

The truth wrought by holiness-cum-pain is a truthfulness that hopes, knowing that new gifts are yet to be given that will transform. This is a truthfulness that insists, always again, that it must be *performed* in public.

—The strange convergence of *holiness*, *pain*, and *truthfulness* insists on concrete bodily practice. Truth given in this holiness is to take the plunge into the neighborhood, the neighborhood of violence and rapacious policy and denial and despair. It is precisely in such neighborly engagement that the God of *ḥesed*, *mišpaṭ*, and *ṣedaqah* shows up as transformative.

These claims arise from the core of our theological tradition:

- God's holiness as active, transformative agent;

- the power of bodily pain allied with active holiness;
- the truth that is generated by holiness-cum-pain;
- the reality of bodily performance of the truth entrusted to us.

It is for such a believing body that the world waits.

4. Finally, as I have pondered Sinai and Solomon and the two great triads, I have thought about Jesus' words to his disciples about anxiety and not having it both ways:

> No one can serve two masters; for a slave will either hate the one and love the other, or be devoted to the one and despise the other. You cannot serve God and wealth.
>
> Therefore I tell you, do not worry about your life, what you will eat or what you will drink, or about your body, what you will wear. Is not life more than food, and the body more than clothing?
>
> Matt 6:24–25

Jesus understands that his disciples were a lot like the world in their several anxieties. He urges them to be different, to be more like trustful creatures (lilies and birds) and less like acquisitive operators. He observes the easy trust and the daily responsiveness of lilies and birds and then he says, in one of his most remarkable utterances:

> Yet I tell you, even Solomon in all his glory was not clothed like one of these.
>
> Matt 6:29

Solomon! Solomon of the great triad of wisdom, might, and wealth! Be unlike Solomon in pursuit of control and domination and safety. Be unlike the triad of Pharaoh, unlike the triad of the national security state, unlike the triad of old certitudes:

> For it is the Gentiles who strive for all these things; and indeed your heavenly Father knows that you need all these things. But strive first for the kingdom of God and his righteousness, and all these things will be given to you as well.
>
> Matt 6:32–33

The cadences of *ḥesed*, *mišpaṭ*, and *ṣedaqah* continue to sound. They are a minority voice of subversion and alternative, and they have been entrusted to such as us.

Chapter 3

FROM VISION TO IMPERATIVE
The Work of Reconstruction

The book of Isaiah, complex as it is, is the longest, most sustained account we have of the ancient city of Jerusalem. It is clear in the book of Isaiah that the city of Jerusalem occupies a central and thick place in Israel's theological imagination, a central and thick place that continues in various forms in contemporary Judaism.

I

The book of Isaiah in recent times has attracted great interpretive attention for this reason. On the one hand, the work of Brevard Childs, Ronald Clements, and Rolf Rendtorff has sought to reengage historical-critical questions in the book from a canonical perspective.[1] Their work concerning the threefold drama of the book of First Isaiah (chapters 1–39), Second Isaiah (chapters 40–55), and Third Isaiah (chapters 56–66) amounts to a near consensus. But Childs, Clements, and Rendtorff, among others, are now impatient

---

1. Brevard S. Childs, *Introduction to the Old Testament as Scripture* (Philadelphia: Fortress Press, 1979), 311–38; Ronald Clements, "The Unity of the Book of Isaiah," *Interpretation* 36 (1982): 117–29; Rolf Rendtorff, *Canon and Theology: Overtures to an Old Testament Theology,* trans. and ed. Margaret Kohl (Overtures to Biblical Theology; Minneapolis: Fortress Press, 1993), 146–69.

with such critical assumptions and seek to read the book as a canonical whole, the shape of which articulates an intentional theological claim. The several parts of the text are indeed intrinsically related to one another and organically connected so that the final form of the text is not a scissors-and-paste job but the knowing act of theological imagination. Like many Isaiah interpreters, I waver between the critical consensus and the postcritical canonical approach, wanting to see the book whole but not doubting that the whole consists in parts that are quite distinct. In what follows you will see how I manage my wavering.

On the other hand, the book of Isaiah has attracted, and continues to attract, attention among Christian readers, because it lends itself readily to a peculiarly Christian reading. For example, John Sawyer has written a book titled *The Fifth Gospel* about the Christian use of the book.[2] The title makes appeal to an early church father who observed that if we lacked the four Gospel narratives we could manage with the book of Isaiah, because it contains all things needful for faith. That judgment, moreover, is more particularly reflected in our liturgical, lectionary appeal to such texts as the royal song of Isaiah 9:2-7 or the song of the Suffering Servant in Isaiah 53.

Indeed, in his last book, Brevard Childs has reviewed the common Christian practice of reading the Song of the Servant in Isaiah 53 in a christological direction, showing that the church's leading interpreters have done so consistently.[3] The final chapter of his book is a lament that postmodern reading—with particular reference to my own

---

2. John F. A. Sawyer, *The Fifth Gospel: Isaiah in the History of Christianity* (Cambridge: Cambridge University Press, 1996).

3. Brevard S. Childs, *The Struggle to Understand Isaiah as Christian Scripture* (Grand Rapids: Eerdmans, 2004).

work—has departed that consensus in a refusal to read the poem christologically.[4] More recently Robert Wilken, in the new commentary series The Church's Bible, has gathered together a huge collection of commentary on the Isaiah text from early Christians. In that collection he shows that they consistently read the book of Isaiah christologically.[5] While I am aware of that sustained propensity and the interpretive history of the church, I have grave reservations about such an approach in our own time on two grounds. First, I doubt if we can honestly read in that way any longer, given what we know critically. It seems to me impossible in any responsible scholarship. Second, even if we can, I am not sure that we should read in any direct christological way, given the long history of supersessionism that preempts the text for our own use. At the very least, any christological reading must attend to the reality that the texts are, in any case, not contained within or exhausted by such an exercise, thus making room for a legitimate reading that is other than our own.

Having recognized the judgment that historical criticism provides restraint on any such Christian reference, my work will make clear that I do not believe that our interpretation should be limited to the possibilities of historical criticism. Thus I am committed to a postcritical reading that allows enormous acts of imagination in reading for our own time and place.[6] For my part, I am not convinced that

---

4. Childs, 291–98.

5. Robert Louis Wilken, *Isaiah Interpreted by Early Christian and Medieval Commentators* (The Church's Bible; Grand Rapids: Eerdmans, 2007). A parallel argument is made concerning the Psalms by Jason Byassee, *Praise Seeking Understanding: Reading the Psalms with Augustine* (Grand Rapids: Eerdmans, 2007).

6. I have in mind the notion of "second naiveté" from Paul Ricoeur, on which see Mark I. Wallace, *The Second Naiveté: Barth, Ricoeur, and the New Yale Theology* (Macon, GA: Mercer University Press, 1990).

an explicitly christological imagination is the best effort; in what follows I will go my own way in postcritical imagination as I seek to read the book of Isaiah toward our own time and place.

II

The book of Isaiah is an interpretive probe about the ancient city of Jerusalem as that city is invested with enormous significance that stays grounded in the political but that soars beyond common politics to the visionary. The book is grounded in the theological-ideological claims of Jerusalem to which the eighth-century prophet Isaiah was apparently committed.[7] As they are given in Israel's text, the political-theological-visionary claims of Jerusalem are two.

On the one hand, the Jerusalem tradition is rooted in the promise to David in 2 Samuel 7 with an unconditional promise to the house of David:

But I will not take my steadfast love from him, as I took it from Saul, whom I put away from before you. Your house and your kingdom shall be made sure forever before me; your throne shall be established forever.

2 Sam 7:15-16 (see Ps 89)

The divine oracle to David is evoked by David's misguided resolve to build a "house for YHWH" in Jerusalem. Chap-

---

7. See the programmatic statement of Gerhard von Rad, *Old Testament Theology*, trans. D. M. G. Stalker (New York: Harper & Row, 1965), 2:147-76; and Robert R. Wilson, *Prophecy and Society in Ancient Israel* (Philadelphia: Fortress Press, 1980), 253-95.

ter 7 follows the account of David's conquest of the city (2 Sam 5:6-10)—the city now named "city of David"—and the transport of the ancient ark to the city (2 Sam 6:1-19).

On the other hand, the Jerusalem tradition is rooted in the account of the dedication of Solomon's temple in 1 Kings 8, the dedication that reaches its liturgic climax in the lyric assertion of YHWH's abiding presence in the Jerusalem temple:

> Then Solomon said,
> "The LORD has said that he would dwell in thick
>   darkness.
> I have built you an exalted house,
>   a place for you to dwell in forever."
>   1 Kgs 8:12-13

Clearly the tradition does not blink at this liturgical accomplishment, even though YHWH, in the oracle of David, has refused such a house (2 Sam 7:5-7; see 1 Kgs 8-9). Thus the *unconditional promise* to the royal house seated in Jerusalem and the *uninterrupted divine presence* in the city together constitute a basis for the theological-visionary claims of the city that have enormous political significance.

This theological-ideological formulation for the city that came to dominate the imagination of urban Israel is, moreover, substantiated and confirmed in the miraculous rescue of the city in 701 BCE from the threat of Sennacherib and the Assyrian army (Isa 37:33-38; 2 Kgs 19:32-37). While the narrative accounts of that rescue in Isaiah and 2 Kings are heavily laden with theological-ideological thickness, no one doubts the historical basis of the rescue. That inexplicable rescue permitted (and required) Israel to conclude that the city was immune from historical threats and vagaries. That conclusion is given primal articulation in the familiar song of Zion, Psalm 46:

> God is our refuge and strength,
>   a very present help in trouble.
> Therefore we will not fear,
>   though the earth should change,
>   though the mountains shake in the heart of the
>   sea;
> though its waters roar and foam,
>   though the mountains tremble with its tumult.
> There is a river whose streams make glad the city of
>   God,
>   the holy habitation of the Most High.
> God is in the midst of the city; it shall not be moved;
>   God will help it when the morning dawns.
>
> Ps 46:1–5

Thus it is my premise that these three memories—*promise to the dynasty*, *divine presence* in the temple, and *divine rescue* from the empire—converge to create an ideological oasis of certitude and confidence in the midst of historical complexities that left the actual city often at risk. It is my thought that the book of Isaiah, whatever may have been the commitments of the eighth-century prophet, moves forward from this ideological formulation. And it does move! It moves according to the historical realities that finally cannot be resisted by ideological resolve. So the book of Isaiah both appeals to the theological-ideological assumptions and places them in question because the facts on the ground tell otherwise. Thus the book of Isaiah and the larger Jerusalem tradition expose this difficult interface between *theological claim* and *lived reality*, a difficult interface that is front and center in the book of Job, a difficult interface that every pastor must face in the form of the theodicy question.

III

The book of Isaiah is an act of Jerusalem imagination. At the outset, I will call attention to the Jerusalem accent in the book only at some seams in the text:
—In chapter 1, at the beginning, the poetry imagines Jerusalem under threat:

> And daughter Zion is left
>   like a booth in a vineyard,
> like a shelter in a cucumber field,
>   like a besieged city.
> If the LORD of hosts
>   had not left us a few survivors,
> we would have been like Sodom,
>   and become like Gomorrah.
> Isa 1:8–9

These verses bespeak two images. The phrase "like a shelter in a cucumber field" perhaps refers to the military situation in which the Assyrian army has leveled everything around and only Jerusalem remains. It is an image of acute vulnerability and threat. These verses end by likening Jerusalem to Sodom and Gomorrah, that is, cities marked by such evil that they are subject to divine destruction. It boggles the mind to think of such poetry uttered in the city or such poetry included in the sacred text. The imagery would feature Isaiah like Jim Wallis in his insistent,

penetrating editorial commentary on the toxic patholo-
gies of our society. That is how the book of Isaiah begins.

—At the turn of the book in chapter 40, the poet has
God answer the suffering and displacement of several generations. The prophet of divine comfort speaks a new word:

> Comfort, O comfort my people,
>   says your God.
> Speak tenderly to Jerusalem,
>   and cry to her
> that she has served her term,
>   that her penalty is paid,
> that she has received from the LORD's hand
>   double for all her sins.
>
> Isa 40:1–2

Now the harshness of God, in poetic rendering, is transposed to "tender speech," or better, the speech is turned
toward the wounded heart of the city.

—The book of Isaiah culminates with an imaginative
rendering of a new Jerusalem:

> For I am about to create new heavens
>   and a new earth;
> the former things shall not be remembered
>   or come to mind.
> But be glad and rejoice forever
>   in what I am creating;
> for I am about to create Jerusalem as a joy,
>   and its people as a delight.
>
> Isa 65:17–18

This is a new city, not the old one restored. Then in 66:12–13, the large vision of Isaiah 65 gives way to the gentle mothering of the city by the God who continues to care for it:

> For thus says the LORD:
> I will extend prosperity to her like a river,
>   and the wealth of the nations
>   like an overflowing stream;
> and you shall nurse and be carried on her arm,
>   and dandled on her knees.
> As a mother comforts her child,
>   so I will comfort you;
>   you shall be comforted in Jerusalem.
>   Isa 66:12–13

If one takes only this quick sketch of an *initial harshness* toward the city (1:8–9), the *divine reversal* (40:1–2), and the *ultimate hope* for the city (65:17–18; 66:12–13), it is clear that the city is imagined with a deep fissure at the center of its narrative, a narrative fissure that is commensurate with the historical reality of destruction and displacement. My accent is on the narrative fissure. These text makers have committed an artistic, imaginative act of construction through which they permit the reader to see the history whole. Given such a shape in the final form, one is bound to notice that this rendering, with a fissure at the center, places the account in profound tension with the ideological claims of 2 Samuel 7 and 1 Kings 8 that persist in political propaganda and liturgical affirmation. In sum, the book of Isaiah constitutes, on the basis of lived experience, a profound challenge to a continuing ideological claim of immunity from historical vagary. The insistence of historical vagary about the city requires that the reader must step outside that ideology and make a different set of responses to the lived reality of the city.

Before I go further, I should be candid about the imaginative leap that I will make in what follows. I believe a text like the book of Isaiah propels such a leap to our own time and place, but every such interpretive leap is, by definition, hazardous.[8] I have already indicated why I do not want to make a direct christological leap. Rather, I want to make an imaginative extrapolation about the *city of Jerusalem* (the proper topic of the book) in a way that does not move directly to the New Testament but may have a larger appeal.[9]

I submit that this rumination on the city of Jerusalem that moves between *ideological claim* and *lived experience* may be taken as a parable of our own Western, or more particularly, U.S. cultural circumstance. That culture, like that of ancient Israel, struggles with the interface of ideology and experience. I am aware of and fully accept that the book of Isaiah is about the real city of Jerusalem, the city that has faced empires and is now the epitome in the world of the struggle over war and peace and land. But I believe the interpretive move I make is legitimate, because every urban culture that is thick with ideological claim (as is our urban culture) invests its city (king and temple; president and Wall Street; the Fed

---

8. I use the term *propel* quite intentionally. Brevard Childs, *Isaiah: A Commentary* (Old Testament Library; Louisville, KY: Westminster John Knox, 2001), 5, 58, 91, 94, 102, repeatedly uses the term *coerce* to characterize the urging of the text. I have no doubt that such a characterization of the text is much too strong and severe, and I take "propel" to be a preferable nuance for the urging of the text.

9. The role of Jerusalem in the New Testament is complex, and I am not able to trace that trajectory here. But one can note on the one hand the weeping of Jesus over the city and on the other hand the anticipation of the new Jerusalem at the end of the Testament. There is no doubt that the New Testament, like the Old, imagines a great fissure in the city.

and an ideologically propelled Supreme Court) with dimensions of ultimacy that run far beyond political-economic reality. Thus I propose a double read so that we hear at the same time that Isaiah is speaking about that ancient Jerusalem and our contemporary context, both of which have a fissure at the center of their story line.

IV

In what follows I will attempt to read Isaiah as a narrative exposé and guide for our urban culture that is now centered in a fissure that has evoked deep ideological crisis. I do not imagine this is the intention of the book of Isaiah, but I believe nonetheless that the text always "means" afresh. A reader in our society, I submit, hearing the text will inescapably move back and forth between that ancient urban crisis and our contemporary crisis. As I read through the text, I will identify six moments that follow, none of which can be skipped over if the interpretive community is to enter the fissure and arrive at possible restoration:

A. Loss (Isaiah 1-39). I will not linger long over this material, except to notice that it is commonly assigned to the eighth-century prophet. But chapters 1-39 are quite complex, and only a little of it can be slotted with the prophet. I make only two comments, as I want to push quickly on in the book.

First, the theme of these chapters is *loss.* It is a rumination on the fact, anticipated in covenantal-prophetic imagination, that a community tied to YHWH but marked by recalcitrance cannot endure. The loss is variously exhibited:

—In chapter 1 we are given a variety of images: aliens who devour (v. 7), bruises, sores, and bleeding wounds (v. 6), loss of kings and reversion to judges (v. 26). In chapter 3, Jerusalem will have "taken away" all its leadership (vv. 2–4) and all its extravagant luxury (vv. 18–23).

—In 5:8–22; 10:1–4; 28:1; 29:1, 15; 30:1; and 31:1, there are a series of "woes" anticipating trouble that is to come as an inevitable outcome of foolish decisions.

—In 39:1–8, the end of the section and an envelope with chapter 1, the future of Jerusalem as displacement is communicated to King Hezekiah. It is conventional—and easy—to slot this material as "divine judgment," and therefore as warrant for destruction. I suggest, however, that the more elemental reality is not judgment but loss. The articulation of "divine wrath," I propose, is a rhetorical strategy for situating and justifying loss.[10] The reality on which the poetry focuses and which faith anticipates is the loss of a known world, the disappearance of security and certitude and legitimacy. As is usual in prophetic discourse, there is a moral dimension to loss because of fractured covenant. That, however, is an interpretive maneuver; what is visible and beyond doubt is that the way that the world was is no more. Prophetic rhetoric, seen in this way, is not so much about scolding or reprimand or shame; the poetry is designed to bring the listener to the reality that the beloved city, the engine of urban ideology, is gone. The literature winds down in chapter 39 in order to make the loss available and beyond denial.

Second, as Marvin Sweeney has seen, chapters 1–12 are organized with four promises offered in 2:2–5; 4:2–6;

10. My colleague Kathleen O'Connor has studied the prophetic oracles of judgment and of promise in relation to theories of post-traumatic stress syndrome. In such a context, the poems of "wrath" can be understood as a coping strategy for the community in its unspeakable loss. See Kathleen M. O'Connor, *Jeremiah: Pain and Promise* (Minneapolis: Fortress Press, 2011).

9:2-7; and 11:1-9.[11] That is, in the final form of the text, the text makers readily look beyond the fissure to newness. In Isaiah 1-39, however, that look beyond is not made a major theme, for a look beyond is premature.

B. Grief (the book of Lamentations). The book of Isaiah moves directly from chapter 39 to chapter 40. But critical scholarship has noticed the caesura from 700 BCE to 540 BCE. While we do not need to take that break historically and chronologically, we do know practically that the break between loss and comfort must be honored and lingered over. One cannot rush to comfort, as every clinical pastoral education supervisor knows. Consequently, we are left with the question, what is available to occupy and assist in the gap between? Critical judgment would now most likely say that between chapters 39 and 40 we must entertain the book of Lamentations and its exquisite, courageous practice of grief.[12] Norman Gottwald has proposed that these poems of grief reflect the voice of those left bereft in the land and not carried away by the Babylonians.[13] These are the ones who every day visited "the site" and were constantly reminded of the loss.

They bring the loss to speech—full, daring speech about abandonment and diminished life. They draw the theological conclusion:

11. Marvin A. Sweeney, *Isaiah 1-4 and the Post-Exilic Understanding of the Isaianic Tradition* (Beihefte zur Zeitschrift für die alttestamentliche Wissenschaft 171; Berlin: de Gruyter, 1988).

12. See Norman K. Gottwald, "Social Class and Ideology in Isaiah 40-55: An Eagletonian Reading," in *The Bible and Liberation: Political and Social Hermeneutics*, ed. Norman K. Gottwald and Richard A. Horsley (rev. ed.; Maryknoll, NY: Orbis, 1993), 329-42; and Patricia Tull Willey, *Remember the Former Things: The Recollection of Previous Texts in Second Isaiah* (Society of Biblical Literature Dissertation Series 161; Atlanta: Scholars Press, 1997).

13. Gottwald, "Social Class and Ideology in Isaiah 40-55," 329-42.

There is none to comfort.
1:2, 9, 17, 21

Voiced grief as a response to loss is now being recovered among us. But Israel knew about voiced grief forever, since its long inventory of complaints and since its initial cry against Pharaoh (Exod 2:23–24).[14] We know about such complaints through the insights of pastoral care; but we have not yet made the move to public grief for public loss, for the loss of the entire fabric of legitimacy and security that is provided by ideology. In the ancient world of David and Solomon's temple, Jerusalem had been guaranteed. And in the United States as God's "most recently chosen people," we have imagined ourselves to be beyond vulnerability. Now loss, loss that evokes regressive speech, that requires savage imagery, that weeps and confesses and accuses, not sure whether this is human failure or divine wrath or aggressive abuse, any of them or all of them.

The fifth poem of the book of Lamentations ends with a choreography of faith, candor, and bewilderment:

In 5:19, *a doxology*:
But you, O LORD, reign forever;
your throne endures to all generations.

In 5:20, *two questions of accusation*:
Why have you forgotten us completely?
Why have you forsaken us these many days?

14. See the fresh and comprehensive discussion of Israel's laments and protests by William S. Morrow, *Protest against God: The Eclipse of a Biblical Tradition* (Sheffield: Sheffield Phoenix Press, 2007).

In 5:21, *a double petition*:
Restore us to yourself, O LORD, that we may be
restored;
renew our days as of old—

Then, in 5:22, an odd ending of *wistful uncertainty*:
unless you have utterly rejected us,
and are angry with us beyond measure.

This final verse is most likely a question, a wondering, and
an uncertainty. Grief insists, but it does not know what
comes next. It waits, but only after it has had its say.[15]

Those in ancient Israel who repeatedly performed
these poems knew that silence could be effectively broken
into the next moment of life. But in our society, with the
fullness of legitimacy deeply in question, we prefer denial
and pretense and we seem, therefore, not to get any further,
not able to move beyond the moment of loss. What Israel
has always known is that *loss grieved* permits newness. And
by contrast, *loss denied* creates social dysfunction and eventually produces violence.[16]

C. Hope (Isaiah 40-55). We are so familiar with chapter
40 coming after chapter 39 that we do not consider that
it need not have been so. The exhaustion of "old things"
does not automatically produce "new things." The move
from chapter 39 to chapter 40 is only by way of the book of
Lamentations, that is, from loss through grief. The grief is

15. On the enigmatic final verse, see Tod Linafelt, *Surviving Lamentations: Catas-
trophe, Lament, and Protest in the Afterlife of a Biblical Book* (Chicago: University of
Chicago Press, 2000), 60-61.
16. On the debilitating, lethal force of silence, see Walter Brueggemann, "Voice as
Counter to Violence," *Calvin Theological Journal* 36 (April 2001): 22-33.

a meditation on "none to comfort." The "none to comfort" of the book of Lamentations is answered in Isaiah 40:1 by "Comfort, O comfort." It is answered by divine response, by the one who hears and honors loss grieved. Chapters 40–55 constitute a divine response to the work of *grief*, work that permits *hope*. Second Isaiah as a response to Lamentations, that is, hope as response to voiced grief, is an instance of Paul's conviction that "suffering . . . produces hope," only I would insist that it must be *voiced* suffering. Where there is no voiced suffering there will not be hope.

Thus our common reading of Second Isaiah—mostly without reference to the loss of chapters 1–39 and without the reference to the voiced grief of the book of Lamentations—seeks to have hope without a context of acknowledged suffering; more than that, it is hope without the hard, painful, preparatory work of loss and grief that makes hope credible. Without the preparatory work, the offer of hope is too easy and too much without context to have transformative power, much like having a Sunday victory without the loss of Friday.

In the long narrative account of Jerusalem offered by the book of Isaiah, and by extrapolation the master account of every failed urban culture, we pause over hope. I will identify four aspects of hope that are central in this poetry and, I believe, central to any hope that has a chance to revive a community of loss and grief. All four of these dimensions of hope are known to us but are worth hearing again in our context of a failed urban culture. In that context, hope takes the form of assurance, contestation, and departure.

The first dimension of hope that responds to loss and grief is an *utterance of newness* that has the rhetorical effect of resituating the listening community. Isaiah 40:1–11 is a new divine address to Jerusalem, an announcement that the displaced city has suffered enough from its recalcitrance and is now at the edge of a new buoyancy. The newness is staged so that it comes from "elsewhere," apparently from the "divine council," a resolve of heaven that does not depend on the conditions or readiness of the earth. The imagery of the highway in verses 3–5 concerns the road home. Of this imagery I notice only that all four Gospels begin with John the Baptist and start out with a quote of this passage, clearly suggesting that Jesus is belatedly a leader on the road home. The exchange among the voices about grass, flowers, and word serves to enunciate divine resolve that is not subject to earthly veto.

My point of accent, however, is in verse 9, after the image of the road home and the word of divine resolve. Verse 9 is a mandate from the divine council, a provision for how to get the news to the earth. It is a strategy for an unexpected, inexplicable intrusion that can only happen by unextrapolated utterance. There is a *commission*: "Get you up." There is an *identification* of the one commissioned: "herald of good tidings." This utterance is the first clear, intentional case of the term *gospel* in the biblical text, gospel as news from outside the system that is sunk in loss and grief. The utterance is surely divine resolve; but it requires a human utterer. The future turns on human utterance, and this is the *substance* of the utterance: "Here is your God," or "Behold your God." It is a pointing to the reemergence of the God of Israel, the God of Jerusalem, in an environment of despair wherein all Jewish possibility had been dismissed by imperial requirement. The Babylonians, by coercion and by liturgical propaganda, had eliminated YHWH from the imaginative horizon of displaced Jews. Now, by daring human artistic utterance, the one dismissed by imperial requirement is back in play in defiance of imperial

requirement. The same assertion is made in 52:7, only the
message is even more specific:

> How beautiful upon the mountains
>   are the feet of the messenger who announces
>   peace,
> who brings good news,
>   who announces salvation,
>   who says to Zion, "Your God reigns."

"Your God" is back in play. More than that, "Your God
reigns," or in liturgical, dramatic fashion, "has just become
king." The assertion in poetic idiom is an act of defiance
and subversion in a simple utterance that overrides the
claims of Babylonian sovereignty. The gospel utterance is a
quote or an allusion back to the Jerusalem liturgy that had
not been forgotten. In that liturgy, in a daring stylized claim
that defied all the facts on the ground, Jerusalem could
declare:

> Say among the nations, "The LORD is king!
>   The world is firmly established;
>   it shall never be moved.
> He will judge the peoples with equity."
> Ps 96:10

The liturgy in Jerusalem made that sweeping assertion,
even though Jerusalem was a small backwater city and
YHWH was the God of a small people. Gospel assertion is
disproportionate in its claim. Now the claim is drawn from
the old liturgy and revoiced in an even more daring context, in a context where YHWH does not at all appear to
be sovereign.

The purpose of such news is to mobilize the displaced to new possibility, to summon them out beyond the assumptions of the empire. The intention of the poetry is to create an edginess that propels listeners out beyond their comfort zone to a wonderment about YHWH in the midst of the more formidable gods of the empire who never intend to create futures.

The statement of YHWH's newly asserted governance puts, and intends to put, Jewish listeners in a bind and summons to a decision. If YHWH is king as you say, what about other claimants? The poetry voices a challenge to assumed imperial reality. In response to that immediate and deeply felt crisis, the poet of hope fashions an imaginative, dramatic scene, a trial among the gods. I will mention two of these poetic scenarios. In Isaiah 41:21–29, we have an imagined trial. In verses 21–24, the court is open to evidence from the imperial gods. They are invited to give evidence of serious Godness. They are invited to tell the future as though they were to cause it. They are invited to tell the past as though it had been their work:

> Set forth your case, says the LORD;
> bring your proofs, says the King of Jacob.
> Let them bring them, and tell us what is to happen.
> Tell us the former things, what they are,
> so that we may consider them,
> and that we may know their outcome;
> or declare to us the things to come.
>
> Isa 41:21–22

Of course, there is no answer. There is a taunting insistence that these gods should act in order to demonstrate their capacity: "do good, do evil, scare us!" No answer!

And then the verdict: Guilty of not being gods:

> You, indeed, are nothing
>   and your work is nothing at all;
>   whoever chooses you is an abomination.
>
> Isa 41:24

And the worshipers, the imperial ilk, are also guilty of being an abomination, the very contradiction of all things holy and divine. This poetic scenario is a vigorous deconstruction of imperial power, inviting the listeners to reconsider their assumption that the empire merits attention or loyalty.

A pause in the poem, a pause in the trial proceedings. Then YHWH testifies to YHWH's own capacity to take initiative:

> I stirred up one from the north, and he has come,
>   from the rising of the sun he was summoned by
>   name.
> He shall trample on rulers as on mortar,
>   as the potter treads clay.
> Who declared it from the beginning, so that we
>   might know,
>   and beforehand, so that we might say, "He is
>   right"?
> There was no one who declared it,
>   none who proclaimed,
>   none who heard your words.
>
> Isa 41:25–26

The poet points to Cyrus, from Persia (Iran), the one from the north. But the trial does not concern Cyrus. It concerns the God who takes credit for international upheaval.

YHWH does not mind a bit of self-regard, for YHWH's people will not recover verve unless they can see that their God is strong enough that they can run a risk of defiance. The assurance of alternative possibility is gospel:

> I first have declared it to Zion,
>> and I give to Jerusalem a herald of good tidings.
>>>> Isa 41:27

When the poem is finished, the final verse 29 refers to the first, negative verdict so that there is no relapse:

> No, they are all a delusion;
>> their works are nothing;
>> their images are empty wind.

The poem is only a poem. It does not accomplish anything metaphysical. It is a bid for imagination. It bids displaced people to host possibility. That hosting, moreover, requires a bold break with unexamined assumptions about the empire and theology that the empire bootlegs along with its political-economic pretensions. The poet opens possibilities for alternative action.

The same drama of contest is staged again in Isaiah 45:20–24. The worshipers of idols are invited to give evidence. I suppose the program would be called among us "Babylonian Idol":

> Assemble yourselves and come together,
>> draw near, you survivors of the nations!
> They have no knowledge—
>> those who carry about their wooden idols,
> and keep on praying to a god that cannot save.

> Declare and present your case;
> let them take counsel together!
>
> Isa 45:20–21a

But the judge will not even wait for the answer to the rhetorical question. The question is, "Who?" The answer that the poet cannot withhold is, "YHWH":

> Who told this long ago?
> Who declared it of old?
> Was it not I, the LORD?
> There is no other god besides me.
>
> Isa 45:21b

Then follows the self-assertion of YHWH, who, by force of utterance, overrides the question, praising righteousness and celebrating triumph:

> Turn to me and be saved,
> all the ends of the earth!
> For I am God, and there is no other.
> By myself I have sworn,
> from my mouth has gone forth in righteousness
> a word that shall not return:
> "To me every knee shall bow,
> every tongue shall swear."
> Only in the LORD, it shall be said of me,
> are righteousness and strength;
> all who were incensed against him
> shall come to him and be ashamed.
> In the LORD all the offspring of Israel
> shall triumph and glory.
>
> Isa 45:22–25

Every knee, every tongue! Every Babylonian knee and tongue. Every knee and tongue of the empire. No knee henceforth would be bowed to empire. No tongue would be used to praise empire. This is only poetry, and poetry does not change the facts. Except that poetry trickles to power and energy is redirected and imagination breaks loose.

D. The contest is reinforced by direct oracles of *assurance*. Now speaks the God who is no longer an agent of settled sovereignty. Now speaks the God who has newly come to power: This God speaks against fear, the very fear by which the gods of the empire have kept all parties on alert against any external threat. But now, so goes the poetic utterance, everything has changed. Displaced peoples need no longer cringe; they can stand tall, reimagine their lives in terms of miracle, and mobilize their energies for new possibility:

> Do not fear, for I am with you,
>> do not be afraid, for I am your God;
> I will strengthen you, I will help you,
>> I will uphold you with my victorious right
>> hand. . . .
> For I, the LORD your God,
>> hold your right hand;
> It is I who say to you, "Do not fear,
>> I will help you."
> Do not fear, you worm Jacob,
>> you insect Israel!
> I will help you, says the LORD;
>> your Redeemer is the Holy One of Israel.
>> Isa 41:10, 13, 14

> But now thus says the LORD,
>> he who created you, O Jacob,

he who formed you, O Israel:
Do not fear, for I have redeemed you;
   I have called you by name, you are mine.
When you pass through the waters, I will be with
     you;
   and through the rivers, they shall not overwhelm
     you;
when you walk through fire you shall not be burned,
   and the flame shall not consume you.
For I am the LORD your God,
   the Holy One of Israel, your Savior.
I give Egypt as your ransom,
   Ethiopia and Seba in exchange for you.
Because you are precious in my sight,
   and honored, and I love you,
I give people in return for you,
   nations in exchange for your life.
Do not fear, for I am with you;
   I will bring your offspring from the east,
   and from the west I will gather you;
I will say to the north, "Give them up,"
   and to the south, "Do not withhold;
bring my sons from far away
   and my daughters from the end of the earth—
everyone who is called by my name,
   whom I created for my glory,
   whom I formed and made."

                                    Isa 43:1–7

Do not fear, or be afraid;
   have I not told you from of old and declared it?
   You are my witnesses!
Is there any god besides me?

> There is no other rock; I know not one.
>
> Isa 44:8

The assurances I mention—the word of the gospel, the refutation of the failed gods, and the nullification of fear—culminate in an *assurance of human agency* with transformative power. The poetry of hope does not float in the sky but gets down to cases. The poetry, before the church arrived at the cunning rhetoric of *homoousia*, finds a way to link the resolve of heaven to the possibility of earth:

> ... who says of Cyrus, "He is my shepherd,
> and he shall carry out all my purpose";
> and who says of Jerusalem, "It shall be rebuilt,"
> and of the temple, "Your foundation shall
> be laid."
>
> Isa 44:28

The destiny of Jerusalem is linked to the designation of Cyrus. This statement of amazing specificity comes as a series of first-person participles for YHWH that begins with creation and moves to the concrete target of failed Jerusalem that will become revived Jerusalem. In poetic interpretation Jerusalem is not a "heavenly city." It is an earthly city that requires human agency. For that reason,

> Thus says the LORD to his anointed, to Cyrus,
> whose right hand I have grasped
> to subdue nations before him
> and strip kings of their robes,
> to open doors before him—
> and the gates shall not be closed.
>
> Isa 45:1

Imagine, a *goy* as anointed, as Messiah, as Christ. Here is a promise that the members of the failed urban economy have *bodied* possibility.

E. This hope is, however, not an easy assurance. For that reason, hope as assurance becomes hope as *contestation*, a culmination that we have already seen in the trial scenes. Contestation is required because Babylon continues to be visibly present and strong. Beyond that, Babylon had a deep grip—a death grip—on the imagination of the Jews. They could not imagine outside the purview of the empire. And so the poet takes on the empire. What a statement, *poet versus empire*! The contest is Isaiah 46 is a *theological* one, between the gods. The Babylonian gods are portrayed in Isaiah 46:1–2 as pitiful gods, weak and ineffective, who need to be carried:

> Those who lavish gold from the purse,
>   and weigh out silver in the scales—
> they hire a goldsmith, who makes it into a god;
>   then they fall down and worship!
> They lift it to their shoulders, they carry it,
>   they set it in its place, and it stands there;
>   it cannot move from its place.
> If one cries out to it, it does not answer
>   or save anyone from trouble.
>   Isa 46:6–7

By contrast, YHWH is a God who carries:

> Even to your old age I am he,
>   even when you turn gray I will carry you.
> I have made, and I will bear;
>   I will carry and will save.
>   Isa 46:4

The contrast invites to decision.

The theological contest of chapter 46 is matched by the *political* challenge in chapter 47. The poet can imagine the proud empire now humiliated and reduced to slavery (vv. 1–5). The ground for the anticipated abasement of the empire is that the empire entrusted by God to punish the Jews had failed to show them mercy:

> I was angry with my people,
> I profaned my heritage;
> I gave them into your hand,
> you showed them no mercy;
> on the aged you made your yoke exceedingly
> heavy.
>
> Isa 47:6

Well, empires do not major in mercy. I can imagine the protest of Nebuchadnezzar: "You never said anything about mercy." And YHWH responds, "You should have known: I am a God of mercy, especially toward my people." Nebuchadnezzar may be a smart military guy; but he is a failure at theology, as is every empire. Every empire imagines it is autonomous and unrestrained:

> You said, "I shall be mistress forever,"
> so that you did not lay these things to heart
> or remember their end.
>
> Now therefore hear this, you lover of pleasures,
> who sit securely, who say in your heart,
> "I am, and there is no one besides me;
> I shall not sit as a widow
> or know the loss of children."

. . . .
You felt secure in your wickedness;
    you said, "No one sees me."
Your wisdom and your knowledge
    led you astray,
    and you said in your heart,
      "I am, and there is no one besides me."
Isa 47:7–8, 10

All such imaginings of autonomy on the part of the empire constitute a theological miscalculation. After all of that miscalculation, so says the poet, there is still YHWH the God of mercy, YHWH the God who engages in poetic utterance, YHWH who counters empire in mercy that makes futures.

    F. The theological contest of Isaiah 46 and the political contest of Isaiah 47 should have left the displaced Jews breathless and ready to decide. It is not enough, however, just to be comforted to assurance and by contest. The listeners must act. So after assurance and contest, there is summons to *departure.* That is why the poetry has begun with a highway. You have to go! The poet, in the ongoing story line, now addresses his audience with urgent imperatives:

Rouse yourself, rouse yourself!
    Stand up, O Jerusalem,
you who have drunk at the hand of the LORD
    the cup of his wrath,
who have drunk to the dregs
    the bowl of staggering.
Isa 51:17

Awake, awake,
    put on your strength, O Zion!
Put on your beautiful garments,

O Jerusalem, the holy city;
for the uncircumcised and the unclean
    shall enter you no more.
Shake yourself from the dust, rise up,
    O captive Jerusalem;
loose the bonds from your neck,
    O captive daughter Zion!
                                        Isa 52:1-2

Depart, depart, go out from there!
    Touch no unclean thing;
go out from the midst of it, purify yourselves,
    you who carry the vessels of the LORD.
For you shall not go out in haste,
    and you shall not go in flight;
for the LORD will go before you,
    and the God of Israel will be your rear guard.
                                        Isa 52:11-12

The displaced are on their way home! They are dressed in celebrative clothes, having shaken off the lethal pressures of the empire. They are to be holy, that is, singularly devoted to the journey out led by YHWH. They are first-class passengers and need not go in haste as they did in Egypt. They will be safe on the journey, because YHWH goes before and behind—but they have to depart.

The poetry of Second Isaiah ends with a jubilant vision of departure:

For you shall go out in joy,
    and be led back in peace;
the mountains and the hills before you
    shall burst into song,

and all the trees of the field shall clap their hands.
Instead of the thorn shall come up the cypress;
    instead of the brier shall come up the myrtle;
and it shall be to the LORD for a memorial,
    for an everlasting sign that shall not be cut off.

Isa 55:12-13

The going out is not stressful. There is joy; there is shalom. There is celebration by all the creatures, so glad to see these human creatures now returning to their proper destiny freely away from the empire. This concluding statement about the applause of the other creatures harks back to the anticipation of 40:5 that all flesh shall see it together. They see the departure from empire, and they sing and dance.

It is all good news . . . but you have to go! Israel has always been departing empire. That is how it began back in Egypt and that is how Nebuchadnezzar became the dominant metaphor for imperial power vis-à-vis the peculiar destiny of Israel. That has been the summons of Jesus to his people since his first "follow me." He summoned away from all old regimes into the new regime that he inaugurated. To make a large, imaginative move, I suggest that it is the task of followers of this gospel in our society—who live in the totalitarian regime of military consumerism with all of its hopes and violences and anxieties—to depart. The departure is not a geographical one as Second Isaiah imagines with his "highway"; the departure is never primarily geographical, for one can change places and still appeal to the same powers of domination. Clearly these articulations of hope—*challenge, assurance, contestation, departure*—are all rhetorical strategies for a departure that is essentially liturgical and imaginative. The possibility is for life lived in an alternative frame of reference organized around a counter loyalty. Thus I complete my movement through Second Isaiah. I do not suggest that the script of Isaiah 40–55, placed canonically, is a generic script. It is a script for a particular time and place, a particular community in a particular empire.

But, of course, we take it as "Scripture," as a disclosure from elsewhere, as a gift that keeps on giving. For that reason, I suggest that while not generic, the script is paradigmatic and may be given concrete replication at other times and places. Consequently, it has occurred to me that the sequence of

> loss discerned,
> grief expressed,
> hope as newness and summons,
> hope as assurance,
> hope as contestation, and
> hope as departure

may be a way to practice evangelical faith in an urban economy that has failed as clearly as the old Jerusalem had failed. I line it out in this way because it is this paradigmatic scripting of crisis that has been peculiarly entrusted to us, and I have no doubt that it is not only faithful to the gospel but elementally true to bodily communal reality. The processive narrative movement from old to new resonates with the deepest human reality; and it cannot be short-circuited.

The matter is all the more urgent, I believe, because the immense force of empire continues its lethal enterprise, refusing to notice the failed fabric of social reality all around. The continuing force of empire specializes in denial that is propelled by euphemisms that misdescribe and by hopes for conforming despair that have no energy for dissent and alternative. The force of empire

- counts *loss* as simply the cost of doing business;
- wants *grief* to be voiced quietly and be over with—or not at all;
- dismisses *hope* as fantasy;
- gives *assurances* of security and well-being that ring false;
- offers totalism that allows no *contestation*; and
- imagines no *departure* because we are already there!

The book of Isaiah as a paradigmatic script of invitation speaks an alternative. Its embrace of Cyrus makes clear that the poetry does not live in a zone of romantic reality. It knows about the reach of empire and entertains that a counterempire under Cyrus can be benign and positive. Thus the poets of Jerusalem sketched out Persian rule as an alternative. But any possible read of empire is in terms of YHWH's rule and purpose, and that requires critical acts of hope and departure.

V

So they departed. Or at least some departed, likely the elite or the fanatics, those who had leverage for an alternative. They became the principal bearers of Judaism that is, to some extent, a product of the Babylonian venue. They departed, dancing to the lyrics of Second Isaiah with eager longing.

When they came back to the imagined home city, they did not find king or temple or walls or economy. They found shambles and so they, like their Babylonian counterparts, sat down and wept (Ps 137:1; Neh 1:4). Their grief was not yet finished. Then, having wept, they moved into the script of Isaiah 56-66, that is, Third Isaiah. It is remarkable that Third Isaiah, not unlike the book of Lamentations, has not been much studied among us. Given our new situation of faith in a Western economy and government that has failed to deliver on elemental promises, I judge that the recovery of Isaiah 56-66 is as important as the recovery of the book of Lamentations.

When we arrive at Isaiah 56-66, the big surprise is that the community is addressed by urgent imperatives to act. This is a contrast to the lyrics of Isaiah 40-55 that are fundamentally indicative assurance. The move from the *indicative* to the *imperative* is what happens when displaced folks reenter and reengage the failed urban fabric. As they departed on the poet's highway home, they could not simply come home, fit in, and settle. There was nothing left of the infrastructure into which to fit. So they are summoned by this poetry to the hard work of reconstruction. This, as one may guess from my title, is the burden of my presentation. From Isaiah 56-66 I make an interpretive connection to our own time and place of evangelical obedience in a failed urban economy. There will not be, as there was not then, any "return to normalcy," as Hananiah had anticipated (Jer 28:3-4). What is required now is initiative-taking actions, local and public, that create anew the capacity to sustain human community and the parallel capacity to maintain an ecosystem that honors all of creation. Of course, we cannot know ahead of time, as they did not know ahead of time, what is required. What we do know and can see in this text is that hard thought and resolved work are required out beyond our comfort zone. I recognize, moreover, that as we take Isaiah 56–66 as our guide, other texts and other perspectives urged otherwise.[17] I will for now consider only this text. I have selected five accent points from this rich poetry:

1. Isaiah 56:1-2. The poetry of Third Isaiah begins in 56:1-2 with what Rolf Rendtorff suggests is a theme or mantra for the whole:[18]

> Thus says the LORD:
> Maintain justice, and do what is right,
> for soon my salvation will come,
>   and my deliverance be revealed.
> Happy is the mortal who does this,
>   the one who holds it fast,
> who keeps the sabbath, not profaning it,
>   and refrains from doing any evil.

The first words are imperatives: *maintain justice, do right.* The phrasing looks back to Isaiah 1:21–26. In that opener, the poet remembers how Jerusalem was at the beginning:

> How the faithful city
>   has become a whore!
> She that was full of *justice*,
> *righteousness* lodged in her—
>   but now murderers!
>   Isa 1:21

---

17. Paul D. Hanson, *The Dawn of Apocalyptic* (rev. ed.; Philadelphia: Fortress Press, 1979), has traced the way in which competing voices of interpretation stand side by side in the text.

18. Rolf Rendtorff, "Isaiah 56:1 as a Key to the Formation of the Book of Isaiah," in *Canon and Theology*, 181–89.

And the poet awaits an "afterward" for the city:

> And I will restore your judges as at the first,
>   and your counselors as at the beginning.
> *Afterward* you shall be called the city of
>   *righteousness*,
>   the *faithful* city.
>
> Isa 1:26

Our verses in chapter 56 are the "afterward" of reconstruction. The imperative is based on an assurance of divine deliverance. The first step on the way to the new city of justice and right is the generic summons to shun evil and the single covenantal reference to Sabbath. I have come to think that for those of us inured to empire Sabbath rest is the most urgent and difficult command, because empires depend on restless productivity. The mandate that begins the poetry is to disengage.

2. *Isaiah 56:3-8.* The first challenge in reconstruction is to determine *membership:* Who belongs? Who gets to the table? Who has a say? Who counts? There were those who, informed by ancient texts, imagined a community of "pure Jews," and one can see the work of this tradition in the function of Ezra. But not here. Here is a different advocacy urging inclusion of foreigners who lack the "pure seed" and eunuchs who lack "good genitalia":[19]

> For thus says the LORD:
> To the eunuchs who keep my sabbaths,

---

19. See Frederick Gaiser, "A New Word on Homosexuality? Isaiah 56:1-8," *Word & World* 14 (1994): 280-93.

> who choose the things that please me
> and hold fast my covenant,
> I will give, in my house and within my walls,
> a monument and a name
> better than sons and daughters;
> I will give them an everlasting name
> that shall not be cut off.
> And the foreigners who join themselves to the LORD,
> to minister to him, to love the name of the LORD,
> and to be his servants,
> all who keep the sabbath, and do not profane it,
> and hold fast my covenant—
> these I will bring to my holy mountain,
> and make them joyful in my house of prayer.
>
> Isa 56:4–7a

This is a quite remarkable assertion, imagining that all willing parties are welcome to the enterprise of reconstruction.

It should not surprise us that questions of membership surface when the infrastructure fails. Every church I know is having a dispute about membership concerning all kinds of "foreigners" and the parallel civic conversation concerns all sorts of "immigrants." Of course, the issues are not quite the same, but they are not unrelated.

The requirements for inclusion are there but are not as rigorous as they might be. There is a requirement that the welcome ones "hold fast to covenant," that is, act like a neighbor. And there is a requirement—surprise!—that Sabbath be kept, because Sabbath is the key mark of existence outside imperial productivity. The demands are there just as they are there in the decision of Acts 15. But they propose, just like Acts 15, a large welcoming membership. The welcome is so large that

> my house shall be called a house of prayer
>> for all peoples.
>>> Isa 56:7b

The God who presides in this house is the *great gatherer:*

>> Thus says the Lord GOD,
>>> who *gathers* the outcasts of Israel,
>> I will *gather* others to them
>>> besides those already *gathered.*
>>>> Isa 56:8

This is the God who belatedly will set the table and say,

>> Come from the East and the West,
>>> from the North and the South,
>> and gather around the table of the Lord.

In the task of reconstruction, the issue of membership must be revisited, because the old distinctions of in and out are no longer adequate.

3. Isaiah 58:1-14. Membership is for the sake of *worship*. Worship is crucial, because it is an act of communal imagination that responds to the new sovereign, and it lines out reality in an alternative way. It does not surprise that there was in this old text a dispute about worship. And surely there were in the conversation punctilious Episcopalians and ferocious Presbyterians and intransigent Baptists and Quakers who thought that they had no "form" but vigorously defended their "no form." But the poet urges that worship must be rethought, even against the tradition. The poet observes that too much covenantal worship is self-indulgence that is, in itself, a violation of neighborliness:

> Look, you serve your own interest on your fast day,
> 　and oppress all your workers.
> Look, you fast only to quarrel and to fight
> 　and to strike with a wicked fist.
> Such fasting as you do today
> 　will not make your voice heard on high.
> 　　　　　　　　　　　　　　　　　Isa 58:3b–4

That worship is self-referential and has on the screen neither the God who outflanked the empire nor the neighbor who remains unnoticed.

We are, of course, familiar with the new worship that is recommended:

> Is not this the fast that I choose:
> 　to loose the bonds of injustice,
> 　to undo the thongs of the yoke,
> to let the oppressed go free,
> 　and to break every yoke?
> Is it not to share your bread with the hungry,
> 　and bring the homeless poor into your house;
> when you see the naked, to cover them,
> 　and not to hide yourself from your own kin?
> 　　　　　　　　　　　　　　　　　Isa 58:6–7

But we do not sense the bite of it without the preceding verses. The new worship concerns the construction and practices of neighborliness of the most elemental kind. The new worship looks advantage and disadvantage square in the face and urges economic gestures that bind haves and have-nots together. The accent is on praxis, thus echoing the remarkable statement of Jeremiah:

> Are you a king
> because you compete in cedar?
> Did not your father eat and drink
> and do justice and righteousness?
> Then it was well with him.
> He judged the cause of the poor and needy;
> then it was well.
> Is not this to know me?
> says the LORD.
>
> Jer 22:15–16

Knowledge of God is acknowledgment of neighbor. *Love of God* is *love of neighbor* (1 John 4:20–21). Obviously one can take this as conventional progressivism. But I suspect it is more radical than that. It is an insistence that the love of God happens in praxis, not in thought or in piety, and that "knowledge of God" is a relational reality, a point well recognized by John Calvin: "All right knowledge of God is born of obedience."[20]

The other thing that strikes me about this remarkable text is a series of "if-then" rhetorical elements:

- In Isaiah 58:6–9a, the "if" of a proper fast is implied. The "then" concerns the presence and response of God to an obedient people.

---

20. John Calvin, *Institutes of the Christian Religion* 1.6.2 (ed. John T. McNeill; trans. Ford Lewis Battles; 2 vols.; Library of Christian Classics 20; Philadelphia: Westminster, 1960), 1:72. Note that Abraham Heschel, *Who Is Man?* (Stanford: Stanford University Press, 1965), 111, comes to a parallel judgment: "I am commanded . . . therefore I am."

- In verses 9b–12, there is a double "if" with reference to a yoke that is heavy, thus echoing verses 6–7. The "then" that follows concerns God's guidance in restoration of the city:

> . . . then your light shall rise in the darkness
>   and your gloom be like the noonday.
> The LORD will guide you continually,
>   and satisfy your needs in parched places,
>   and make your bones strong;
> and you shall be like a watered garden,
>   like a spring of water,
>   whose waters never fail.
> Your ancient ruins shall be rebuilt;
>   you shall raise up the foundations of many
>   generations;
>   you shall be called the repairer of the breach,
>   the restorer of streets to live in.
>
> Isa 58:10b–12

- In verses 13–14, there is a triple "if" with a "then" of buoyant triumph. The three "then" clauses show that God's gift of well-being is contingent on neighborly behavior by the community. It is clear that the case for neighborly worship becomes crucial for all else that follows. It is unmistakable that worship here is understood as no separate zone, but it is an element in the large practice of neighborly restoration and reconstruction.

4. Isaiah 61:1–4. The accent is on the *economy*. These familiar verses probe the phrases "year of the LORD's favor" and "vengeance of our God":

> The spirit of the Lord GOD is upon me,
> because the LORD has anointed me;
> he has sent me to bring good news to the oppressed,
>   to bind up the brokenhearted,
> to proclaim liberty to the captives,
>   and release to the prisoners;
> to proclaim the year of the LORD's favor,
>   and the day of vengeance of our God;
>   to comfort all who mourn.
>
> Isa 61:1–2

The subject of concern is the oppressed, the broken-hearted, the captives, and the prisoners. It is everywhere judged that these phrases concern the practice of the jubilee year wherein the functioning of the economy is subordinated to the requirements of the neighborhood. Thus the third agenda of reconstruction, along with membership and worship, is economic transformation. The old teaching of the jubilee year and the year of release operate on the assumption that the rich and the poor, creditors and debtors, are bound together in a common destiny that precludes conventional economics. There is no doubt, according to prophetic critique, that old Jerusalem had been a venue for conventional economics in which the strong dominated the weak. The poet insists on an alternative future, an alternative that is voiced in the rhetoric of three "insteads":

> . . . to provide for those who mourn in Zion—
>   to give them a garland *instead* of ashes,
> the oil of gladness *instead* of mourning,
>   the mantle of praise *instead* of a faint spirit.

> They will be called oaks of righteousness,
>> the planting of the LORD, to display his glory.
>>>>> Isa 61:3[21]

The "insteads" of verse 3 result in the reconstruction of verse 4:

> They shall build up the ancient ruins,
>> they shall raise up the former devastations;
> they shall repair the ruined cities,
>> the devastations of many generations.

The poem is a daring appeal to old texts that are quoted and affirmed, in contrast to the poem on membership in Isaiah 56 that seems to refute old texts. The sum of all these texts in Isaiah indicates a lovely, supple imaginative process that can tilt tradition and engage it in a variety of ways, all of those ways committed to an alternative. This text is an invitation and summons to proactive engagement that moves beyond the shambles of the city in fresh ways.

5. Isaiah 65:17-25. After these four summons to *justice, membership, worship,* and *economics,* I mention the great visionary poem of Isaiah 65:17-25 concerning new heaven and new earth. It is clear that for all the urgency of the imperatives, the imperatives must be kept within a frame of *vision.* The vision in Isaiah 65 is soaring in its possibility for heaven, for earth, and for Jerusalem. But the newnesses that soar in this poetry are notably public and material. My best guess is that all the urgency of the vision is as an anti-

---

21. The three "insteads" in this verse function as a counterpoint to the five negative "insteads" in 3:24. Whether intentional or not, the juxtaposition of the two clusters of uses nicely provides an epitome of the drama of the book.

dote to the totalizing capacity of the empire to co-opt vision for the status quo. Isaiah 56–66 insists that there is nothing ordinary about the possible; but it requires folks to step out in generative, engaged ways.

VI

It will be clear that my large leap from this paradigmatic script to our time and place takes it as a guide for evangelical obedience in our contemporary world. I believe it is impossible to overstate the defining nature of the empire of force among us, if empire is understood as a political, economic, military, ideological practice of self-security and control.[22] It is not clear that life can be construed beyond empire; but the poets have to try. The poets, because they are poets, never arrive there, for their *poetry* would then become *program*. That, however, does not render the poetry as a failure or as an irrelevance. It only affirms that alternatives to the lethal reductionism of empire require imagination and courage and staying power. In that ancient world, it was required that *old Jerusalem be relinquished* and *new Jerusalem be undertaken.* It is no less required now that there be *relinquishing* and *undertaking.* Those who act in this way will do so at the behest of the poets who may eventually be seen as Spirit led. The news since Isaiah 1:26 is that for the fallen city there is an "afterward." The poets teach us how to embrace "afterward"—by loss and grief and hope, eventually to act.

---

22. On the "empire of force," see James Boyd White, *Living Speech: Resisting the Empire of Force* (Princeton: Princeton University Press, 2006).

SCRIPTURE INDEX